CU00704666

CONSTITUTION

For The
New
Socialist
Republic In
North America

(Draft Proposal)

From the Revolutionary Communist Party, USA

Copyright © 2010 RCP Publications

Published in October 2010 by RCP Publications
Printed in USA

ISBN: 978-0-89851-007-2

RCP Publications
P.O. Box 3486
Merchandise Mart
Chicago, Illinois 60654-0486
revcom.us

Introductory Explanation: On the Nature, Purpose and Role of This Constitution (Draft Proposal)

This Constitution (Draft Proposal) is written with the future in mind. It is intended to set forth a basic model, and fundamental principles and guidelines, for the nature and functioning of a vastly different society and government than now exists: the New Socialist Republic in North America, a socialist state which would embody, institutionalize and promote radically different relations and values among people; a socialist state whose final and fundamental aim would be to achieve, together with the revolutionary struggle throughout the world, the emancipation of humanity as a whole and the opening of a whole new epoch in human history–communism–with the final abolition of all exploitative and oppressive relations among human beings and the destructive antagonistic conflicts to which these relations give rise.

In order to bring this new socialist state into being, it would be necessary to thoroughly defeat, dismantle and abolish the capitalist-imperialist state of the USA; and this in turn would only become possible with the development of a profound and acute crisis in society and the emergence of a revolutionary people, in the millions and millions, who have the leadership of a revolutionary communist vanguard and are conscious of the need for revolutionary change and determined to fight for it. To work for this objective–to hasten while awaiting the emergence of these necessary conditions, with the goal of revolution and ultimately communism clearly in mind–is the strategic orientation of the Revolutionary Communist Party, USA. And, as one important part of giving life to and carrying out this strategic orientation, we are publishing this "Constitution for the New Socialist Republic in North America (Draft Proposal)": as a contribution to a process in which growing numbers of people are seriously considering and grappling with whether, how, and in what form there could be a real alternative to the present capitalist-imperialist system and the unspeakable suffering and depredations it imposes on the great majority of people in the world, on humanity as whole, as well as on the environment and the webs of interconnected species which inhabit this earth; to provide a more concrete sense of the basic nature, structure and functioning of the socialist society, and its government, envisioned here, and the principles and objectives underlying and guiding this; and to enable people to see, sharply outlined, what is in reality the radical difference between the society and government envisioned here and the capitalist-imperialist system which currently rules in this country and exercises domination over the world as a whole, with such terrible consequences.

The term "New Socialist Republic in North America" has been chosen not because that would necessarily be the name of such a socialist society, brought into being through revolution in this part of the world (the formal name would of course be decided at the time of the actual establishment of such a socialist state); rather, this term is utilized in order to emphasize that this is intended as a proposal for the Constitution of a socialist state <u>as it would have been newly brought into being</u>, in the first stages of its existence, with the victory of the revolution that would have put an end to the imperialist USA and replaced it with a new, revolutionary society on the road of socialism. And, while we have sought to indicate here, as much as possible, the basic principles, institutions, structures, and processes which would characterize this new socialist society, and particularly the functioning of its government, much of the specific features of this would naturally be influenced by the situation that existed at the time of the establishment of this new socialist state–including factors such as the size of the territory that had been liberated from the imperialists (and other reactionaries) and consolidated as the territory of the new socialist state, and what overall situation prevailed, particularly in terms of the struggle between revolutionary and reactionary forces, in this part of the world, and in the world overall, at the time of the founding of this new socialist state. Some of this is spoken to in the Constitution (Draft Proposal) that follows, but there are clearly aspects of such a future situation which can be anticipated only in broad terms, and others which may arise which cannot at all be anticipated now. Nevertheless, it has been our purpose, and we have striven to the best of our ability, to put forward as clearly as possible the basic principles that would be embodied in a Constitution for a new socialist state in North America, and much of the specific ways in which these principles would be applied, in order to enable and encourage people to engage, in a serious and substantive way, with the vision that is put forth here of this new socialist state and the potential for a radically different society and world that it represents. For, again, that is our purpose in publishing this Draft Proposal: to stimulate, as broadly as possible, such serious and substantive engagement with this Draft Proposal, and vigorous discussion and debate about what it puts forward as the kind of society and world to be not only imagined but actively struggled for.

A final point. As a Draft Proposal for a Constitution for a new socialist state, this document focuses on and is primarily concerned with addressing the purposes, nature, objectives, and functioning of the government in this new society and does not attempt to discuss to any great depth the philosophical-ideological and political-strategic thinking regarding the necessity and basis for, and the means for bringing into being, such a state. For more background in relation to this, we strongly recommend the talks and writings of the Chair of our Party, Bob Avakian, as well as other Party publications, including: *Birds Cannot Give Birth to Crocodiles, But Humanity Can Soar Beyond the Horizon; Revolution and Communism: A Foundation and Strategic Orientation; Constitution of the Revolutionary Communist Party, USA;* and *Communism: The Beginning of a New Stage: A Manifesto from the Revolutionary Communist Party, USA.*

Revolutionary Communist Party, USA, October 2010

CONSTITUTION FOR THE NEW SOCIALIST REPUBLIC IN NORTH AMERICA

(Draft Proposal)

This Constitution consists of a Preamble and six Articles:

Preamble

The New Socialist Republic in North America could only have been brought into being as a result of heroic, self-sacrificing struggle carried out by millions and millions of people who had been forced to live under a system of exploitation and oppression in the former United States of America; who could no longer tolerate the continual outrages and injustices perpetrated by the system of capitalism-imperialism and the structures and institutions of power and repression which enforced all this with violence and brutality as well as lies and deception; who refused to any longer accept that this was the best possible society and world, and were increasingly aware of and inspired by the possibility of a radically different and better society and world; and who therefore rose up, with the leadership of the Revolutionary Communist Party, to defeat, abolish and dismantle the imperialist system in the former USA and its institutions and apparatus of repression and violence. At the same time, this new socialist state could only have resulted from a whole process of revolutionary work and struggle, in the realm of theory as well as practical-political activity, by the Revolutionary Communist Party, acting as the vanguard of the revolutionary process, to enable both the Party itself and growing numbers of broader masses to prepare for and then to seize on the emergence of a revolutionary situation, to defeat and dismantle the forces of the old, oppressive order, and establish the new socialist state. In this whole process, the interaction and mutual reinforcement between the vanguard role of the Revolutionary Communist Party—with its theoretical basis in the science of communism and the further development of this science through the new synthesis brought forward by Bob Avakian—and the growing consciousness and increasingly determined struggle of masses of people, constitute a decisive element in the success of the revolution and the founding of the new, revolutionary socialist state. The Constitution for the New Socialist Republic in North America continues and gives further expression and initiative, in the conditions of the new society, to the fundamental principles and motive forces that constitute the basis for the establishment of this new socialist state.

In contrast to the way in which the capitalist-imperialist state serves and enforces the interests of a small ruling group of exploiters, the New Socialist Republic in North America, with the continuing leadership of the Revolutionary Communist Party, bases itself on, and proceeds from, the fundamental interests of those most bitterly exploited and oppressed under the old system, and the masses of people broadly, and provides the means for them to play an increasingly widening role in the exercise of political power and the functioning of society in accordance with those interests–in order to carry forward the struggle to transform society, with the goal of uprooting and finally eliminating all oppressive and exploitative relations among human beings and the destructive antagonistic conflicts to which these relations give rise.

This is a process and goal which, fundamentally and in the final analysis, can only be achieved on a global scale, with the advance to communism throughout the world. The orientation and principles of this state, as embodied in this Constitution, are internationalist: While giving due emphasis to meeting the material, intellectual and cultural needs of the people within this state, on a continually expanding basis, and to promoting the further transformation of this society to continue uprooting social inequalities and remaining aspects of exploitation and oppression, the socialist state must give fundamental priority to the advance of the revolutionary struggle, and the final goal of communism, throughout the world, and must adopt and carry out policies and actions which are in accordance with and give concrete effect to this internationalist orientation.

Regardless of differences, even very great and qualitative differences, in their political structures, institutions and guiding principles, all states have a definite social content and class character: they are an expression of the prevailing social relations, and most fundamentally the economic relations (relations of production), which have a decisive and ultimately determining role in regard to how the particular society functions and is organized. The state serves to protect and expand those relations and to enforce the interests of the social group–the ruling class–which holds the dominant position in society, as a result of its role in the economy, and in particular its ownership and control of the major means of production (including land, raw materials and other resources, technology and physical structures such as factories, and so on). In capitalist society, it is the capitalist class which holds this dominant position: the government structures and processes–and above all the organs of the <u>state</u> as an instrument of class rule and suppression (the armed forces, police, courts and prisons, the executive power, and the bureaucracies)–are controlled by this capitalist class as a means of exercising its rule over society and its repression of forces whose interests are in significant opposition to, and/or which resist, its rule. In short, all states are an instrument of <u>dictatorship</u>–of a monopoly of political power, concentrated as a monopoly of "legitimate" armed force and violence–exercised by, and in the interests of, one class or another. Any democracy which is practiced in this situation is democracy on the terms of, and fundamentally serving the interests of, the ruling class and its exercise of dictatorship. And it will remain the case that there will be a state, and that the state will constitute a dictatorship of one kind or another, serving the interests of one ruling class or another, so long as society is divided into classes (and other groups) with interests that are fundamentally antagonistic–a division rooted in the underlying social relations, and above all the production relations, which predominate in the given society.

The New Socialist Republic in North America is, like all states, a form of dictatorship–the <u>dictatorship of the proletariat</u>–which means that, in its essential character and its basic principles, structures, institutions and political processes, it must give expression to and serve the fundamental interests of the proletariat, a class whose exploitation is the engine of the accumulation of capitalist wealth and the functioning of capitalist society and whose emancipation from its exploited condition can only be brought about through the communist revolution, with its goal of abolishing all relations of exploitation and oppression and achieving the emancipation of humanity as a whole. In accordance with this, the governing bodies and processes of this socialist state, at all levels, must be vehicles for the furtherance of the communist revolution; and, as a key dimension of this, they must provide the means for those who were exploited and oppressed in the old society–and were effectively locked out of the exercise of political power and the governance of society, as well as the spheres of intellectual endeavor and working with ideas overall–to increasingly take part in these spheres, with the aim of continually transforming society in the direction of communism. All this is given expression through the principles and provisions, and the institutions, structures and processes which are set forth and provided for in this Constitution.

At the same time, the New Socialist Republic in North America is a continuation of the strategic orientation of United Front under the Leadership of the Proletariat, in the conditions of the new society which has been brought into being through the revolutionary struggle. This means that, while it must be recognized that the essential nature, and the basic principles and processes, of this Republic are oriented in accordance with the interests of the proletariat, as a class, in the most fundamental and largest sense–abolishing all relations of exploitation and oppression through the advance to communism throughout the world–the struggle to achieve this goal cannot be, and will not be, carried out simply by PROLETARIANS, as some idealized "perfect embodiment of communist principles," and in some uniform and linear sense. As the new synthesis brought forward by Bob Avakian has given emphasis to, the process of making revolution, and then continuing the revolution in the new socialist state toward the final goal of communism, must involve the active participation of broad ranks of the people, of different strata, and will proceed through many different "channels," involving many diverse forces among the people in many different spheres of human endeavor, not only those more directly political or relating more directly, at any given time, to the functioning and objectives of the leadership of the revolution and the new socialist state; and the orientation and aim, consciously taken up by growing numbers of the people, must be to work so as to enable all this to contribute, in the final analysis, to the struggle to further transform society in the direction of communism.

In keeping with this orientation and these objectives, the principle of "solid core, with a lot of elasticity" must be applied. This means that, on the one hand, there must be a continually expanding force in society, with the revolutionary communist party as its leading element, which is firmly convinced of the need to advance to communism and deeply committed to carrying forward this struggle, through all the difficulties and obstacles; and, on the basis of and at the same time as continually strengthening this "solid core," there must be provision and scope for a wide diversity of thinking and activity, among people throughout society, "going off in many different directions," grappling and experimenting with many diverse ideas and programs and fields of endeavor–and once again all this must be "embraced" by the vanguard party and the "solid core" in an overall sense and enabled to contribute, through many divergent paths, to the advance along a broad road toward the goal of communism. This orientation and approach is embodied in the Constitution for the New Socialist Republic in North America.

The New Socialist Republic in North America is a multi-national and multi-lingual state, which is based on the principle of equality between different nationalities and cultures and has as one of its essential objectives fully overcoming national oppression and inequality, which was such a fundamental part of the imperialist USA throughout its history. Only on the basis of these principles and objectives can divisions among humanity by country and nation be finally overcome and surpassed and a world community of freely associating human beings be brought into being. This orientation is also embodied in the various institutions of the state and in the functioning of the government in the New Socialist Republic in North America.

The oppression of women arose together with the emergence of exploitative class divisions among human beings thousands of years ago, has been carried forward and become deeply entrenched in all societies ruled by exploiting classes, and was a marked feature of the imperialist United States of America and its domination and influence in the world. Abolishing and uprooting all this is one of the most important objectives of the New Socialist Republic in North America. This is expressed not only in full legal equality between women and men, but beyond that in the declared orientation and policy of this Republic to overcome all "tradition's chains" embodied in traditional gender roles and divisions, and all the oppressive relations bound up with this, in every sphere of society, and to enable women, as fully as men, to take part in and contribute to every aspect of the struggle to transform society, and the world, in order to uproot and abolish all relations of oppression and exploitation and emancipate humanity as a whole.

In an overall sense, and in accordance with the principles and provisions of this Constitution, the Revolutionary Communist Party provides leadership to the state and its key institutions. Members of the Party, at all levels, dedicate themselves to upholding, propagating and implementing the Constitution of the Party as well as the Constitution of the New Socialist Republic in North America. While there are differences between these two Constitutions–as aspects of the viewpoint, objectives and responsibilities of Party members, embodied in the Party Constitution, extend beyond what is set forth in the Constitution for the New Socialist Republic–there is a fundamental unity between the principles of the two Constitutions; the Party, and all its members, are accountable to and may not act in violation of, and on the contrary must consistently act on the basis of and in accordance with, the Constitution for the New Socialist Republic in North America.

As historical experience has demonstrated, socialist society will–for a considerable period of time–contain, and in fact regenerate, elements of exploitation, social inequality and oppression, which have been, unavoidably, inherited from the old society and cannot be uprooted and abolished all at once, or soon after the establishment of the socialist state. Further, there is likely to be a protracted period in which new socialist states come into existence in a situation where they are, to one degree or another, encircled by imperialist and reactionary states, which will continue to exert significant influence and force, and may even occupy a dominant position in the world for some time. These factors will, for a long time, repeatedly give rise to forces within socialist society itself, as well as within the parts of the world still dominated by imperialism and reaction, which will attempt to overthrow any socialist states that exist and restore capitalism there. And historical experience has also demonstrated that, as a result of these contradictions, forces will emerge within the vanguard party itself, including at its top levels, which will fight for lines and policies that will actually lead to the undermining of socialism and the restoration of capitalism. All this underscores the importance of continuing the revolution within socialist society, and of doing so in the overall framework of the revolutionary struggle throughout the world and with the internationalist orientation of giving fundamental priority to the advance of this worldwide struggle toward the achievement of communism, which is only possible on a world scale—and the importance of struggle within the party itself, as well as in society as a whole, to maintain and strengthen the revolutionary character and role of the party, in keeping with its responsibilities to act as the leadership of the continuing revolution toward the final goal of communism, and to defeat attempts to transform the party into its opposite, into a vehicle for the restoration of the old, exploitative and oppressive society.

With the final abolition of class divisions and all other exploitative and oppressive relations among people, throughout the world, there will still remain a need for government, in the sense of providing an organized framework for decision-making and the administration of the common affairs of the human beings who make up society, on its various levels, and for the pursuit by individuals and groups within society of their particular inclinations, preferences and concerns within the overall cooperative functioning and ethos of society. But the need and the basis for a state—as an organ of class rule and of suppression of classes and groups antagonistically opposed to the ruling class—will have been eliminated, and the state will have been abolished. In these conditions, the basis and need for an organized group of people exercising a disproportionate influence in the sphere of government, and in society overall, will also have been surpassed, and vanguard parties, with a special role in the governance of society, will have been eliminated. Advancing to such a communist society, bringing into being the conditions that make that possible and achievable—through continuing revolutionary struggle to transform all spheres of society, within a particular socialist state and in the world as a whole—is the fundamental aim of the socialist state and of the vanguard party which plays a leading role within that state. While recognizing the complex and protracted nature of the struggle to overcome the relations and divisions which make a state and a vanguard necessary, the socialist state and its leading party must, at every stage in this process, not only propagate this goal but promote and give effect to concrete measures which lead in this direction.

The preceding constitutes the basis and foundation for the Articles that follow in this Constitution for the New Socialist Republic in North America.

Article I. The Central Government.

Section 1. The Legislature.

1. The central Legislature in the New Socialist Republic in North America constitutes the law-making body for the Republic as a whole. It shall have the authority to legislate laws for the Republic as a whole, on the basis of and in accordance with the principles and provisions set forth in this Constitution. This shall include the authority to ratify, through a vote of a majority of its members, treaties entered into by the government of the New Socialist Republic in North America–and such treaties, when so ratified, shall become, and shall have the force of, law within this Republic. All laws, including treaties, are subject to review by the Supreme Court, and other courts which may be established and have jurisdiction (see Section 3 of this Article); but unless and until a law passed by the central Legislature has been ruled, by the appropriate judicial body, to be in violation of the Constitution, it shall have the power and authority of law (this shall also apply to laws enacted by legislative bodies, with law-making authority, which may be established in other areas of governance within this Republic). Unless otherwise indicated in this Constitution–or otherwise prescribed by rules and procedures adopted by the Legislature, in accordance with this Constitution–laws passed, and other actions taken, by the Legislature shall require only a simple majority vote.

Laws, as well as other official government documents, shall be published in both English and Spanish. In proceedings of the central Legislature, both Spanish and English may be utilized, with translation from the one language into the other provided simultaneously. If there are areas–and this might apply particularly in certain autonomous regions or areas that may be established–where significant parts of the population have some language other than Spanish or English as their first language, the policy shall be to create the basis so that laws and documents are published in that language and that language may be used in legislative proceedings.

The central Legislature shall also provide for the establishment of the appropriate governmental authority and administration in regions, localities, and other areas and institutions within the New Socialist Republic in North America. (This includes autonomous regions, or other autonomous areas, which may be established where there are significant populations of minority and formerly oppressed nationalities–see Article II, Section 3.)

2. The central Legislature shall be chosen by apportioned popular vote, direct and indirect (see part 3 in this Section). Election to the Legislature shall, as a general rule, be held every five years, after the first such election–which will have been held within six months after the founding of the New Socialist Republic in North America, and will have been organized by a Provisional Governing Council established by the Revolutionary Communist Party. Prior to this first election of the Legislature, laws will have been promulgated, and institutions created to give effect to the laws, and to the governance and administration of the Republic, by the Provisional Governing Council, in accordance with the principles and provisions of this Constitution (which shall also have been adopted by the Provisional Governing Council–see Article V). Upon its election, the first Legislature shall review the laws and other actions taken by the Provisional Governing Council and may, on the basis of and in conformity with this Constitution, revise what has been done by the Provisional Governing Council. The Legislature (or, in the case of the first election to the Legislature, the Provisional Governing Council) shall determine the ratio of elected to electors in the voting for the Legislature, but the size of the Legislature must, in any case, not be more than 500 members nor less than 300. The elected Legislature shall itself certify the validity of the election and of those elected to serve in the Legislature; these decisions of the Legislature, regarding the validity of the election and the standing of those elected, may be appealed to the Supreme Court, but unless and until the decision of the Legislature in this regard is overturned, it shall stand and be in effect. The Legislature, by a vote of 2/3 or more of its members, may also cause an election to be held before five years have expired since the last election for the Legislature.

The first session of each elected Legislature shall be held within two months of the date of the election. The Legislature shall meet at least once a year, and as often as may be deemed necessary by the Legislature itself. As a matter of basic orientation and policy, sessions of the Legislature shall be open to the public, and public awareness of the proceedings of the Legislature shall be encouraged and facilitated; the only exception to this shall be where a reasonable concern regarding the security of this Republic and its people may require non-public proceedings of the whole or parts of the Legislature, but such situations should not be allowed to undermine or fundamentally compromise the general orientation and policy that the proceedings of the Legislature shall be open to and made known to the public. The Legislature may also be called into session by the Executive (see Section 2 of this Article).

After the Legislature has first been elected (within six months after the founding of the New Socialist Republic in North America) and has taken office, it has the authority to determine the specific date of the next election–but, with the exception of circumstances of extraordinary emergency (see Article III), the time between elections to the central Legislature may not be more than five years.

The Legislature shall elect, from among its members, a chairperson to preside during sessions of the Legislature and other officers of the Legislature that it may deem necessary and appropriate for its functioning. The Legislature shall have the authority to establish the rules and procedures regarding its functioning, so long as this is in conformity with this Constitution. The Legislature shall also be empowered to pass measures providing for the livelihood of its members, while they are serving in the Legislature–and the basic standards provided for in this way shall apply more generally to officials of government at various levels and in various spheres–so long as this is in accord with reasonable standards, conforming to those in society generally, and in accord with this Constitution overall.

Those eligible to vote in elections for the Legislature are all the citizens of the New Socialist Republic in North America who have reached the age of 18, with the exception of those who may have been deprived of the right to vote, for life or for a certain designated period, through a lawful process in accordance with this Constitution (in this regard see Section 3 of this Article and especially Article III). All citizens who are eligible to vote shall also be eligible to stand for election to the Legislature and, if elected, to serve in the Legislature for the term for which they are elected.

3. Apportioned popular vote, as the means of election of the central Legislature, shall be organized and conducted in accordance with provisions and procedures established by the Legislature (or, in the case of the first elected Legislature in the New Socialist Republic in North America, by the Provisional Governing Council). But the following shall apply in the voting for the central Legislature:

i. 20% of the total seats shall be determined through votes cast by the organs of government at workplaces, neighborhoods, educational institutions, and other basic institutions of society (these organs of government shall themselves be elected by popular vote–see Article II, Section 2).

ii. 20% of the total seats shall be determined through votes cast by the organs of government in the local areas and regions, including any autonomous regions and autonomous areas that may be established (these organs of government shall also be elected by popular vote–see Article II, Section 1).

iii. 30% of the total seats shall be determined through votes cast through direct popular election, with voting to be conducted by districts, established by the central Legislature (or, in the case of the first elected Legislature, by the Provisional Governing Council) for the purpose of electing this Legislature. Everyone eligible to vote and to serve in the Legislature may stand for election in this process.

iv. 30% of the total seats shall be also determined by votes cast through direct popular election, conducted by districts, in the same manner and with the same eligibility requirements as described in the paragraph above (iii), with the difference that in this process those standing for election will have been recommended by a nominating council established and led by the Revolutionary Communist Party (it shall be the general orientation of this council, and of the Party in establishing and leading it, that wherever and whenever feasible more than one group of candidates shall be nominated and that those nominated reflect a diversity of views, within the overall framework of the principles and objectives set forth in the Preamble and elsewhere in this Constitution).

v. While the Legislature–or, in the case of the first election to the Legislature, the Provisional Governing Council–shall determine the ratio of elected to electors in the voting for the Legislature, the percentages set forth in points i through iv above may not be altered and the total number of the Legislature may not exceed 500, nor be less than 300, members.

vi. Access to government media and other public means of communication shall be made available, on an equal basis, to all those who are candidates for direct election (as set forth in 3,iii and 3,iv above), and a situation shall be fostered where all candidates can have their views and intentions made known in an atmosphere conducive to serious consideration, discussion and debate in regard to the views and intentions of the candidates.

Section 2. The Executive.

1. On the basis of this Constitution and laws passed in accordance with it, the Executive shall have invested in it the authority and necessary powers to adopt and effect policies regarding the operation of government and the direction of society, as well as the defense of this Republic and the security and rights of its people.

2. The Executive shall consist of an Executive Council elected by the Legislature, from among the members of the Legislature, according to rules and procedures the Legislature shall establish for this purpose, through a vote of a simple majority of its members, providing that these rules and procedures are in conformity with this Constitution. This election of the Executive Council shall be the first act of the newly elected Legislature. This must be done with due deliberation but as expeditiously as possible on that basis–within three months of the election of the particular Legislature–and the new Executive Council shall assume office, with the full authority and powers of that office, as soon as it is elected by the Legislature. Until such a new Executive Council is elected by the Legislature and assumes office, the previous Executive Council shall remain in office, with the full authority and powers of that office. (In the circumstances prevailing before

the first election to the Legislature, the authority, powers and functions of the Executive will have been determined and given effect by the Provisional Governing Council, in accordance with the basic principles embodied in this Constitution.)

The size of the Executive Council shall be determined by the Legislature which elects it, keeping in mind that this Council is an administrative, not a legislative, body: It should be large enough to effect the collectivity and division of labor necessary for and appropriate to its functions, but not so large as to be unwieldy and encumbered in its functions. It should be a general guideline that the Executive Council will combine people of different ages and particular experiences, but all members must be of voting age. This Executive Council shall in turn elect, from among its members, its chairperson and any other officers it may deem necessary for and appropriate to its purposes and functions. Once elected, the Executive Council shall hold office until a new Executive Council is elected by the Legislature and takes office. (The Legislature shall have the power to recall the Executive Council. The means for such a recall, and for ensuring continuity of the Executive in the event of such a recall, are discussed below.) The Executive Council itself shall have the authority to determine the term of its chairperson and any other officers it may establish, and it may change this, and may replace such officers, at any time, by a simple majority vote of its members.

The Executive shall be independent of the Legislature, except that it is elected by the Legislature from among the members of the Legislature, and may be recalled, or members of the Executive impeached, by the Legislature. During the time of their participation in the Executive Council, members of this Council shall not serve as members of the Legislature, nor have the right to participate or vote in matters before the Legislature–except that, if a vote in the Legislature should result in a tie, and after repeated attempts to resolve the matter through new votes the result is the same and the Legislature cannot break this deadlock, the chairperson of the Executive Council shall cast the deciding vote in this matter.

The Executive Council shall, as a general rule, serve for the length of the term of the Legislature which elects it, but the Executive Council may be recalled, and a new Executive

Council elected, by the Legislature, during the term of the given Legislature (even before the next election for the Legislature). To recall the Executive Council in this way requires a vote of at least 2/3 of the members of the Legislature, while in the event of such a recall the election of a new Executive Council shall be conducted immediately–within 48 hours–by the Legislature. Until such a new Executive Council is elected and assumes office, the chairperson of the Legislature shall assume responsibility for the executive functions of government, utilizing the institutions and organs of administration that have been established for the functioning of the Executive. To further ensure the continuity of the Executive function, and of government as a whole, the Legislature shall also have established, as one of its first acts– within 48 hours after the Legislature is first in session–the further lines of responsibility, among the members of the Legislature, for the assumption of the executive functions of government, in the event of a recall of the Executive Council or other circumstances in which the existing Executive Council is no longer able to function and the chairperson of the Legislature is unable to assume the Executive responsibility.

In the event of actions which, in its judgment, constitute violations of the Constitution and/or of the law, the Legislature may also impeach members of the Executive Council. To initiate such impeachment proceedings requires the vote of at least 2/3 of the members of the Legislature, and conviction requires the vote of at least 3/4 of the members of the Legislature. In cases of impeachment, a member of the Supreme Court, chosen by it, shall preside over the proceedings. The same basic principles and procedures shall apply with regard to impeachment of members of the Legislature itself, or of the judiciary (in the event of an impeachment proceeding against one or more members of the Supreme Court, however, a member of a court at the next lowest level shall preside). Impeachment is a very serious matter and should not be undertaken except in cases of violation of the Constitution and/or of the law. Upon conviction for impeachment, persons so convicted may not hold any public office for a period of at least 10 years, and after that time must receive the approval of a majority of the central Legislature before they can hold any such office; they may also be prosecuted criminally for violation of the law.

3. At the same time as it is elected–and may be recalled or its members impeached–by the Legislature, the Executive Council also operates on the principle of leadership by the Revolutionary Communist Party. This leadership is exercised not so much and not essentially by a numerical preponderance of members of the Party in this Executive Council–and in fact it is the general orientation and approach of the Party not to seek to dominate the Executive Council, or to effect its influence on this Council, by relying on organizational means and the securing of a majority on the Council. Rather, whatever the number of Party members who may at any given time be elected to and serving on the Executive Council, the Party's leadership of this Council will be effected primarily and essentially through the overall influence in society of the Party's political and ideological line, and more specifically and directly through proposals and recommendations that the Party may make to the Executive Council concerning matters of policy and the general conduct and actions of the Executive Council, and discussion, involving representatives of the Party and of the Executive Council, about these proposals and recommendations, as well as the situation in society and the world as a whole. Such discussions shall be held regularly during the term of the Executive Council, but the role of the Party in this regard is essentially advisory; the Executive Council and its members are under no obligation, legal or otherwise, to adopt proposals and recommendations made by the Party, and the spirit and orientation in which such discussions are held should be one of mutual exploration of problems and concerns and learning from each other. The principle of leadership by the Revolutionary Communist Party, as applied to the Executive Council, shall not be construed or approached in such a way as to conflict with or undermine–but rather shall work in fundamental unity with–the basic principles and provisions which establish in the Legislature the authority and power to elect, and to recall or impeach, the Executive Council and its members, and to be apprised, in a timely way, of matters concerning the work of this Executive Council, the conduct of the government and affairs of state more generally, and the situation in society and the world as a whole, in light of and in relation to the principles and objectives set forth in this Constitution.

4. To carry out its duties in situations of extraordinary emergency, the Executive Council has the authority and the responsibility to call the central Legislature into session (see Article III). It may also, in agreement and coordination with the appropriate officers of the Legislature, call the Legislature into session for some other purpose.

5. The Executive Council shall report on its work, and matters relating to its authority and powers, at least once a year to a session of the Legislature, so as to keep the Legislature informed with regard to these matters. This shall include an accounting of the state of the finances of the government and budgets for the central and regional and other government bodies, with regard to specific needs and for periods deemed necessary and appropriate by the Executive. These budgets shall have effect, on the initiative of the Executive, unless they shall be opposed by a vote of at least 2/3 of the members of the Legislature. Public funds for the functioning of the executive, and for government in general, on the various levels, are accumulated through the state's central and regulating role in the economy and are allocated in accordance with a budget drawn up by the Executive. This budget normally applies to the period corresponding to the length of term of the Executive Council, although in keeping with overall socialist economic planning and the larger needs of the society and government, it may envision and provide for some longer-term expenditures. As all of the funding for the government is based ultimately on the initiative and work, physical and intellectual, of the people, serious and systematic attention must be paid to making the most efficient and productive use of such funds, in accordance with the fundamental interests of the masses of people and in the service of the principles and objectives set forth in this Constitution. The general orientation of the Executive and the government as a whole shall be to avoid, or to minimize as much as possible, debt and operating at a deficit.

6. As an essential point of orientation–and while keeping in mind legitimate security concerns of this Republic and its people–reports made by the Executive Council to the Legislature shall also be made accessible to the general population through various media, and it shall be the basic orientation of the Executive

Council to inform the members of society, in a frequent manner and in such a way as to foster and facilitate the active and increasing involvement of masses of people, on an informed basis, concerning the functioning of government and affairs of state, and generally the process of transforming society and the world in accordance with the principles and objectives set forth in this Constitution.

7. On the basis of this Constitution, and laws established by the Legislature in accordance with the Constitution, the Executive is responsible for–and may establish various bodies, and other means and instrumentalities, under its overall direction, to implement policies regarding–various spheres of government and society, including the following:

A. The Economy.

1. The basic character and objectives with regard to the economy and its development are set forth in Article IV. Here it is important to underline that the development of the economy, along socialist lines, is the foundation for carrying out the functions of government and affairs of state in the interests of the broad masses of people, within the New Socialist Republic in North America and in the world as a whole. The fundamental objective is to carry out the development of the economy and the transformation of economic relations, and relations in society and the world overall, in such a way as to eliminate and uproot all aspects of exploitation and oppression and so that finally the means of production (as distinguished from items of personal use and consumption) become the common property and resource of the whole of society, and ultimately all of humanity, in accordance with the fact that these means of production, and the wealth that is produced in general, are fundamentally the result of the labor, both intellectual and physical, of people throughout the world. With the achievement of communism, throughout the world, ownership of the means of production by the whole people will take place directly, that is, without the need for or the mediation of a state (although, once again, there will still be a need for, and a role of, government, in regard to the economy as well as other aspects of society, as discussed in the Preamble of this Constitution). Within a particular socialist country, before

the goal of communism has been achieved on a world level–and this is particularly so with regard to the early stages of the socialist transition to communism, to which the New Socialist Republic in North America, and the Constitution embodying the principles of this Republic, now correspond–the ownership by society of the means of production will be expressed primarily and most essentially through the medium of the socialist state, and its increasingly predominant role in the ownership of means of production and the overall socialist economy, even as the state itself is being continually transformed in line with and in the direction of the achievement of communism.

2. The development of the socialist economy has as its source and relies upon the initiative and work, intellectual as well as physical, of the masses of people, of the members of society broadly, in conditions which are increasingly freed from relations of exploitation, and with the aim of overcoming all vestiges and aspects of such relations, and the effects of such relations, not only in this society but everywhere on the earth. In accordance with these objectives and this orientation, the state is the central and leading element in the development of the new socialist economy, state ownership of the means of production is the primary form of economic ownership and state planning the primary guideline in the development of the economy–while, as indicated in the principles and objectives set forth in this Constitution, the socialist state is not only already radically different from all previous forms of state which embodied and enforced the interests of capitalists and other exploiting classes, but once again the orientation is to continually transform the state, in relation and in tempo with the transformation of the society, and the world, as a whole, toward the goal of overcoming the divisions which make a state necessary, and to finally create the conditions in which the state can be abolished and replaced by the common association of human beings without distinctions of class or nation, or other relations which embody, or contain the seeds of, exploitation and oppression.

3. In keeping with this orientation and with the predominance of state ownership and state planning in the development of the new socialist economy, one of the principal aims is to eliminate

the ownership of private capital and the resultant relations of exploitation in the form of wage labor; and while, for a fairly long period of time, it will be necessary for people employed in enterprises and other units of the socialist economy to receive remuneration–and to meet their various personal needs, to a significant degree–through the medium of money, it will be possible, and will be the orientation, to eliminate, in a much shorter period of time, conditions and situations in which individuals are forced to work for other individuals who own private capital. Accordingly, the private ownership of means of production and other capital, and the hiring of wage labor by owners of private capital, shall be prohibited, except on a transitional basis, on a small scale and in conditions specifically provided for in the overall plans and policies for the development of the socialist economy and within the limits set by these plans and policies. With regard to small-scale owners of means of production, while incorporating their operations within the overall plans and policies for the development of the socialist economy, the orientation shall be to develop these operations in the direction of joint cooperation with the economic functions of the state and, in a relatively short period of time and in relation to the overall development of the economy and transformation of society, to buy out such private operations, integrate their property into the overall resources of the state, and integrate their former owners into the ranks of working people employed in state-owned enterprises and other, collective and cooperative, units of the economy.

Within the overall framework of socialist economic development, in which state ownership and state planning predominate, there shall also be, for a certain period, the development of cooperative and collective forms of ownership and economic functioning, on various levels and involving varying numbers of people, and this may include the merging of former units of private ownership and capital into such cooperative and collective forms. With regard to this dimension of the economy as well, the orientation and aim shall be to increasingly transform these cooperative and collective forms in the direction of larger-scale ownership and eventually incorporate them into the state-owned sector of the economy, as part of the overall development toward the ownership by all of society of the means of production. This orientation shall be applied with regard to agriculture as well as industry and other segments of the economy, while due attention must also be paid to the particularities of each segment of the economy as well as to differences with regard to region and other factors which may influence the particular ways in which this orientation, and policies flowing from it, should be practically applied.

B. The Environment.

1. In the development of the socialist economy, and in the overall functioning of the government, within the New Socialist Republic in North America and in its international relations, not only must the fundamental orientation and principles of proletarian internationalism be consistently adhered to and applied, but this has special and urgent relevance with regard to the environment. In addition to–and in a dimension far beyond–damage that had been done to the environment in previous periods of history, the fundamental dynamics and the overall operation of the capitalist-imperialist system in this era–not least the wars and other massive destruction this system repeatedly gives rise to and continually causes–have created an environmental crisis constituting a genuine and increasingly severe emergency, and this is being and will be continually heightened and exacerbated, for so long as the system of capitalism-imperialism continues to dominate, or to exert significant influence and force in, the world.

The establishment of the New Socialist Republic in North America, through the defeat of the imperialist state of the USA, while it could not have occurred without the unleashing of further violent and destructive acts on the part of that outmoded imperialist state, nevertheless represents a truly gigantic stride toward the emancipation of humanity and with regard to the ability to more frontally and comprehensively confront and address the critical environmental emergency threatening humanity and the other species and ecosystems (the complex webs of interacting and interrelating life) on this earth. In full recognition of this, the New Socialist Republic in North America, in its development of a socialist economy, in all spheres of government and social activity, and in its international relations, will apply itself–and the initiative, knowledge, energy and creativity of the masses of people who make up and are the backbone of this Republic–to addressing this environmental emergency, in its various dimensions, and will seek out the ways to do so through increasing cooperation and common endeavor with scientists, and people from all walks of life, in every part of the world, struggling and joining with others in struggle to overcome barriers that are placed in the way of such efforts by the operation of the capitalist-imperialist system and the functioning of imperialist and other reactionary states.

2. Already, in the period before the revolution that led to the establishment of the New Socialist Republic in North America, the Revolutionary Communist Party (in what was then the imperialist United States of America) published a special issue of its newspaper, *Revolution* (issue #199, April 6, 2010) which analyzed the extent, depth and urgency of the environmental crisis at that time and the fundamental elements and principles of a program for addressing this crisis. One of the distinguishing features of the New Socialist Republic in North America is its determination to apply the principles set forth at that time by the Revolutionary Communist Party–and what has been learned since, with further developments with regard to the environmental crisis and in the world more generally–in order to contribute all it can to solving this environmental crisis and, to the greatest degree possible, reversing its terrible and manifold effects, and to ushering in a new era in which human beings and their society can truly be fit caretakers of the earth.

C. Defense and Security.

1. The basic components and structures of the armed forces and militia and other organs of public defense and security of the New Socialist Republic in North America will have been brought into being through the course of the revolutionary struggle for power, once the conditions for that struggle had emerged: the development of an acute revolutionary crisis and the emergence of a revolutionary people, in the millions and millions, who have the leadership of a revolutionary communist vanguard and are conscious of the need for revolutionary change and determined to fight for it. With the establishment of this Republic, these institutions of public defense and security will be further developed in accordance with their essential purpose and role: to defend

and safeguard the New Socialist Republic in North America and the security and rights of its people, in furtherance of the aims of this Republic and in support of the masses of people in carrying forward the revolutionary transformation of society, and contributing as much as possible to this transformation throughout the world.

2. In keeping with this purpose and role, and in accordance with its internationalist orientation, the New Socialist Republic in North America will dismantle all remaining bases of the former imperialist USA in other countries and will renounce all treaties and agreements, military and otherwise, which were imposed by that imperialist state on other countries and peoples or which in any case served to impose and enforce the domination of the imperialist USA. The New Socialist Republic in North America renounces all wars of aggression and domination, and all occupation of other countries in pursuit of such domination and aggression, and will not station its forces, nor establish bases, in another country, except in circumstances where this is clearly in accord with the wishes of the masses of people in that country and where such action would actually be a manifestation of the internationalist orientation and other fundamental principles and objectives set forth in this Constitution and would contribute to the advance of revolutionary struggle in the world in accordance with these principles and objectives.

3. The New Socialist Republic in North America will not develop, and will not use, nuclear weapons or other weapons of mass destruction. It will wage a determined and many-sided struggle to rid the world of all such weapons–and it will do this as part of the larger, overall struggle to defeat and dismantle all imperialist and reactionary states and forces and to advance toward the achievement of communism, throughout the world, which will finally make it possible for the desires and dreams of countless human beings throughout history, and the fundamental interests of humanity, for a world without war, to at long last be realized.

4. In every aspect of their functioning and operations, the armed forces, militia and other organs of public defense and security of the New Socialist Republic in North America shall act in

accordance with the principles set forth in this Constitution, and laws based on this Constitution (including treaties which become law as a result of the provisions set forth herein). In circumstances of war (or other situations in which there are hostilities) this shall apply to the treatment of prisoners and others detained under the jurisdiction and control of the armed forces, militia and other institutions of public defense and security: no prisoner or any other person may be tortured or subjected to other forms of cruel and unusual punishment, nor treated in any other way which violates the high standards which must be maintained in accordance with the nature, purpose and role of these institutions of defense and security, as set forth in this Constitution.

5. In recruiting members of the armed forces, and other public defense and security organs, priority will be given to those–citizens and others who have been granted residency within this Republic–who, on the basis of dedication to the cause of the revolution and the principles and goals set forth in this Constitution, volunteer to join. Where and to the extent that it deems it necessary for the defense of this Republic and public security, the Legislature may pass a law instituting a draft of able-bodied female and male citizens and residents of the New Socialist Republic in North America who are of the appropriate adult ages; but, in these circumstances as well, priority and reliance will be placed on recruiting volunteers, in accordance with the criteria and standards indicated here. Militias shall be established at the various levels of society–regions, including autonomous regions (and other autonomous areas) which may be established, localities and basic units and institutions–drawing their members from persons 18 years or older, with the aim of providing military training and organization, as well as ideological and political orientation, to broad and growing ranks of the people, on the basis of and in accordance with what is set forth in this Constitution. (With regard to the right of individuals to bear arms, see Article III.)

6. The armed forces, militia and other organs of public defense and security shall be under a system of overall leadership combining the central Executive Council and the Revolutionary Communist Party, with the Party having the ultimate leader-

ship responsibility and role. To this effect, a Commission for Defense and Security shall be established, with its members selected through consultation between the Executive Council and the Revolutionary Communist Party. This Commission shall oversee the operations of the armed forces, militia and other organs of public defense and security, including their doctrine and operational principles; it may make changes in the overall structure and chain of command of these institutions, as well as the positions of different personnel within this chain of command, particularly at its higher levels. The work of this Commission shall be overseen and reviewed by the Executive Council, in consultation with the Party, and in what should be rare occasions where agreement cannot be reached through such consultation in matters concerning the role and functioning of the armed forces, militia and other organs of public defense and security, the Party shall have the final say.

7. The leadership of the Revolutionary Communist Party, with regard to the armed forces, militia and other organs of public defense and security, is a key means of combatting tendencies for these institutions, which embody a concentration of the political power of the state, to turn into a force not only standing above but in antagonistic relation to the masses of people and the principles and objectives set forth in this Constitution. While Party leadership cannot be a guarantee against such a development–and in fact there must be continuing struggle throughout the Party itself, as well as the larger society, to combat tendencies for the Party to turn into its opposite, changing from the vanguard of the revolution into a force of counter-revolution, becoming an instrument for the restoration of capitalism and the consequent exploitation and oppression of the masses of people–it remains the case that, so long as the basic viewpoint, orientation, program and policies (the line) of the Party is revolutionary, the leadership of the Party will be crucial in maintaining and further developing the armed forces, militia and other organs of defense and security as safeguards of the most fundamental and largest interests of the proletariat, protectors of the safety and rights of the people, and key instruments in the advance on the road of socialism toward the final goal of communism.

The leadership of the Revolutionary Communist Party with regard to the socialist state overall is expressed and effected in a concentrated way through the revolutionary communist line of the Party and policies and actions that are concrete manifestations and applications of that line. With regard to the armed forces, militia and other institutions of public defense and security, the leadership of the Party is realized not only in the fact that, as spoken to above, the Party has the ultimate say in matters relating to these institutions, but even more decisively in the ideological and political influence of the Party's line throughout the ranks of these institutions (as well as in society more broadly). To this end, the Party, in consultation with and acting in coordination with the appropriate leadership at the various levels of these institutions, shall establish (and maintain and develop where they may already exist) mechanisms through which the Party can promote education and ideological and political orientation, in all the departments and at all the levels of these institutions, regarding the nature and purpose of these institutions, as key instrumentalities of the New Socialist Republic in North America, in accordance with what is set forth in the Preamble and elsewhere in this Constitution, including in this Section.

8. At the same time as they are under the overall and ultimate leadership of the Revolutionary Communist Party, the army and militia and other organs of public defense and security are accountable to the Constitution of the New Socialist Republic in North America and may not, under any circumstances, act in violation of this Constitution; on the contrary, they must, in all circumstances, including those of extraordinary emergency, act in a manner consistent with and conforming to the principles and provisions set forth in this Constitution and laws which are adopted in accordance with it. The armed forces and the militia and other organs of public defense and security at the various levels shall, under the leadership of the Commission for Defense and Security, and with the ultimate leading role of the Party, establish their own regulations and procedures and codes of conduct and justice, so long as these are in conformity with the Constitution of the New Socialist Republic in North America (and, in addition to any ways in which they may be liable to action under these regulations and procedures and codes of conduct and justice, members of the armed forces, militia and other organs of public defense and security may be prosecuted in the

regular ["civilian"] courts for any violations of laws of the New Socialist Republic in North America established in accordance with this Constitution).

9. The practice and promotion of equality between women and men, and between different nationalities, cultures and languages, shall be upheld and applied in the armed forces, militia and other institutions of public defense and security. Discrimination against people on the basis of sexual orientation is prohibited in these institutions (as well as in society as a whole–see Article III).

10. The principles, procedures and functioning of the armed forces, militia and other organs of public defense and security shall promote the closest possible unity between those with leadership responsibility and the broader ranks. Differences in rank will exist among the armed forces, militia and security forces but these should be simplified as much as possible, and outward expressions of such distinctions must be minimized (for example, with regard to uniforms, insignia and other designations of rank, as well as with regard to the attitude and conduct of people with higher rank and authority) in accordance with the principles of these institutions of public defense and security and of this Constitution as a whole. Things such as saluting and "yes-sir-ing" are contrary to the orientation, purpose and spirit of these institutions in the New Socialist Republic in North America, as they tend to encourage slavish and not conscious discipline and allegiance. Cohesion and discipline within these institutions are of great importance and must be consistently adhered to and developed, and it is the duty of everyone in their ranks to carry out orders in a timely way, and especially so in conditions of war or extraordinary emergency. But the means must be fostered and applied to have, throughout the ranks, ongoing discussion of the nature and purpose of these institutions of public defense and security; and the atmosphere must be created and consistently maintained where–in the appropriate ways, in conformity with the principles set forth here and regulations, procedures, and codes of conduct that may be adopted by these institutions in accordance with this Constitution–members of these institutions, at every level, feel free to, and are encouraged to, raise questions, disagreements and criticisms with regard to policies and actions of these institutions

and persons holding positions of higher leadership and authority within them.

Beyond that, the orientation and principles of these institutions, and policy and action flowing from them, must promote relations of unity and comradeship not only among their own ranks but also between them and the broad masses of people in society at large. Members at all levels of these institutions of public defense and security must never forget–and there must be the continual promotion of education, discussion and struggle throughout these institutions, and among all their members, to instill and deepen the understanding and orientation–that these institutions exist to safeguard the victories of the revolution, and the new socialist state which was brought into being through this revolution, on the basis of the most arduous and self-sacrificing struggle of masses of people; to contribute to the further advance of that revolution; and to safeguard the security and rights of the people and help to create a situation and an atmosphere in which growing ranks of the people will be enabled to, and will, take part in the process of grappling, in an active way, in a lively atmosphere, with the vital matters concerning affairs of state, the governance and direction of society, and the conditions and future of humanity.

D. Justice and the Rights of the People.

1. The responsibility for the enforcement of the laws and the defense of the Constitution by the organs of public security resides with the Executive Council, with the overall and ultimate leadership of the Revolutionary Communist Party. The Executive Council is also responsible for establishing, and providing the necessary funds and resources for, bodies which will carry out the prosecution of those who are accused of violating the law. This shall include the establishment–in consultation with the executive at other levels of government that are established in accordance with this Constitution–of the institutions which are responsible for the prosecution of violations of laws in those other areas of governance and legal jurisdiction, within the overall New Socialist Republic in North America (see also Article II).

At the same time, the Executive Council also has responsibility for safeguarding the rights of the people, as established on the basis of this Constitution, and specifically for overseeing the operation of the organs of public security, and those responsible for the prosecution of crimes, to ensure that their policies and actions are in accord with the Constitution and the law and with the rights of the people established on that basis (see Section 3 of this Article and Article III). The Executive Council shall also create such bodies as are, in its judgment, necessary to carry out these responsibilities and further these ends.

2. As a key part of providing the fullest protection for the rights and liberties of the people, and more specifically the defense of their rights in situations where they are accused of crimes–as well as in other proceedings where citizens or residents of this Republic are confronting the government as a legal adversary and have the right to legal representation–there shall be a Department of Legal Defense and Assistance, which shall be funded by the government, as part of the overall budget prepared by the Executive Council, but which shall in every other way be independent of, and operated independently of, the government. Branches of this Department of Legal Defense and Assistance, funded out of the overall government budget, shall also be established in the various regions, including any autonomous regions (or other autonomous areas) which may be established, and other areas of governmental responsibility and administration. The funds and resources allotted for this Department of Legal Defense and Assistance, including its various branches, must be at least equal to those provided, at the corresponding levels of government, for the prosecution of crimes. This Department of Legal Defense and Assistance, and its various branches, shall, with the resources provided by the government, establish the necessary personnel, structures and procedures in order to carry out the functions assigned to it by–and within the overall framework of what is set forth in–this Constitution.

E. International Relations.

1. The development of the United States of America as a powerful capitalist-imperialist state was, for centuries, marked by and based on expansion through slavery, conquest, domination and plunder, with genocidal dimensions to all this–spreading by this means its system of exploitation throughout much of

North America and large parts of the world, with devastating consequences for those who directly fell victim to its juggernaut of oppression, and for humanity as a whole. The defeat and dismantling of the imperialist state of the USA, its far-reaching tentacles of suffocating exploitation and its massive machinery of death and destruction, will have struck a tremendous blow for the liberation of people everywhere in the world and greatly strengthened the basis for making further advances and leaps in the revolutionary struggle throughout the world toward the final goal of communism. Still, much more remains to be done to win further victories, as well as to defend what has already been won, and the New Socialist Republic in North America must meet this challenge and shoulder this responsibility.

2. In its international relations, the New Socialist Republic in North America will give priority to overcoming the terrible legacy of exploitation and depredation by the imperialist USA and to contributing all it can to the advance to a world in which all conquest, plunder, and domination, and all exploitation, have been finally ended. It will approach relations in the international arena, including those with the other states, in accordance with these principles and priorities. The New Socialist Republic in North America must, most fundamentally, be a base area and source of support and inspiration for the world revolution. (In this connection, and in regard to what follows here, see also part C above in this Article and Article IV.) This will find expression, first and foremost, in support for revolutionary forces, movements and struggles throughout the world, with the aim of advancing to a communist world as the fundamental guiding principle.

3. Relations with remaining imperialist and other reactionary states at any given time must not be in fundamental conflict with, and must be subordinated to, the development and transformation of the New Socialist Republic in North America itself along the road of socialism, and above all the advance of the revolutionary struggle throughout the world, toward the goal of communism. Treaties and agreements regarding trade and other aspects of relations between states must be in accordance with this orientation and these principles. (As set forth in Section 1 of this Article, all treaties and similar agreements entered into by the government

of the New Socialist Republic in North America must be approved by the central Legislature, by a simple majority vote, and when so approved they have the effect and force of law.)

4. With other socialist states that may exist, or come into being, the orientation of the New Socialist Republic in North America shall be to develop relations of mutual aid and support, and mutual efforts in assisting the revolutionary struggle throughout the world.

5. With regard to inequalities between nationalities and regions (as well as other inequalities) within the New Socialist Republic in North America which resulted from the historical development and functioning of the imperialist United States of America, the New Socialist Republic in North America shall give important priority, in the development of the economy, the structure and functioning of the government, and in other ways, to overcoming this inequality, as a crucial part of developing this new socialist state in accordance with the principles and objectives set forth here and elsewhere in this Constitution.

F. Education.

1. Education in the New Socialist Republic in North America shall be based in accordance with, and contribute to, the principles and objectives set forth in this Constitution. All education shall be public education, provided for financially through the allocation of funds from the central government and other levels of government, under the overall direction of the Executive Council of the central government.

Education providing not only for literacy and other basic skills and abilities but also for a grounding in the natural and social sciences, as well as art and culture and other spheres, and in the ability to work with ideas in general, shall be provided, at government expense, and shall be compulsory for all youth (both citizens and residents) within the New Socialist Republic in North America, in accordance with policy and guidelines that shall be adopted by the appropriate government bodies for this purpose. Advanced education, combining specialization with the continuance of overall, well-rounded learning, shall also be provided at government expense for those who meet the criteria and standards for this more advanced education, as set forth in policy and guidelines developed by the appropriate government bodies, in accordance with the principles and objectives embodied in this Constitution. And, on the basis of and in tempo with the development of the socialist economy and society overall, it shall be the orientation of the state to provide such advanced education to increasing numbers of the adult population. In furtherance of these ends, museums relating to history, natural history and science, art, and other spheres, as well as other institutions and programs, shall be developed in accordance with the basic principles and objectives set forth here, and shall be made available widely to the population as a whole.

Education, while valuing and giving expression to the circumstances and atmosphere that are favorable and conducive to learning and intellectual pursuit, shall avoid and combat an "ivory tower" environment and mentality and, on the contrary, shall promote interchanges between students and the broader ranks of the people, on the basis of and in keeping with the principles and policies of the educational system. At the same time, education at all levels shall combine intellectual pursuits with various kinds of physical labor, in ways and forms that correspond to and are appropriate for students of different ages and different levels of development, in order to foster the development of new generations of people with well-rounded experience, knowledge and abilities, and as part of working to transform the relation between intellectual and physical work so that this no longer constitutes the basis for social antagonism.

Overcoming, in society (and ultimately the world) as a whole, such antagonism relating to the division between mental and physical work, which is deeply rooted in the development of societies marked by oppressive and exploitative relations and which is itself a potential source of such relations, shall be a concern of the state overall, and attention shall be paid to this in all spheres of society.

2. One of the most important purposes of the educational system in the New Socialist Republic in North America is to enable students (and the people broadly) to learn deeply about the reality of, and the basis for, the oppression of whole peoples, and the domination and oppression of women, in the former

imperialist USA and throughout the world where societies have been founded on exploitation and ruled by exploiting classes–and, on this basis, to become deeply dedicated to and actively involved in the fight to uproot and eliminate all such relations of inequality and oppression. This shall also be the approach with regard to discrimination against and oppression of people based on sexual orientation, which is closely bound up with traditional gender roles and the oppression of women.

3. As an expression of the multi-national, multi-lingual character of the New Socialist Republic in North America, of the history and current composition of the population of this Republic, and of its internationalist orientation and its goal of overcoming and abolishing all inequality between nationalities and cultures, all education shall be conducted in Spanish and English equally, as a matter of government policy. (And, as indicated in Section 1 of this Article, all laws and other official documents of the government shall be published in both languages.) In any areas where significant sections of the population have another language as their first language, efforts and resources shall be devoted to providing education in that language as well. Along with this, it shall be the goal of the state to encourage and assist people in society as a whole to become fluent in both English and Spanish and, as far as possible, to acquaint themselves with other languages, particularly those spoken by significant groups within the population of this Republic, as well as languages spoken by significant numbers of people in other parts of the world.

4. The educational system in the New Socialist Republic in North America must enable people to pursue the truth wherever it leads, with a spirit of critical thinking and scientific curiosity, and in this way to continually learn about the world and be better able to contribute to changing it in accordance with the fundamental interests of humanity. To this end, in the study of human society and its historical development, and in the social as well as the natural sciences in general, the pursuit of the truth, through the accumulation of facts and empirical evidence and the synthesis of this through logical reasoning and rational discourse, including the testing of ideas against reality, shall be the objective and standard. Scientific and other theories which have

met these criteria and have been clearly confirmed and validated through the scientific method (such as evolution, which is one of the most soundly confirmed and well established facts in all of science) shall be presented as what they are–true and valid understanding of reality–and shall serve as a foundation from which to proceed in further learning about and changing the world, while at the same time the ongoing application of the scientific method shall be fostered and supported in order to continue learning more about the dynamics of processes such as evolution and the natural-material world in general. The dialectical materialist understanding that all of reality consists of matter in motion, of various kinds, and nothing else, and the application of this understanding and approach to all spheres of natural and social science shall be the foundation and "solid core" of education. At the same time, as an application of "elasticity on the basis of a solid core," there shall be provision for other, opposing viewpoints to be presented, including by ardent advocates of those viewpoints, as a part of the overall curriculum and general education. In this regard, too, the orientation of pursuing the truth and the determination of whether something does or does not correspond to objective reality as the standard and criterion of truth, should be applied, while at the same time encouraging an atmosphere in which new and unconventional ideas are not suffocated or suppressed but instead are seriously engaged, with a recognition of the fact that it has been the case throughout history, and will remain the case in the future, that truth is often "in the hands of a minority" and that this applies in particular to newly discovered understanding of reality.

Education in the realm of art and culture in particular, but also as a matter of overall orientation and approach with regard to education in general, should foster an atmosphere that promotes and stimulates imagination, creativity and a wide diversity of artistic and other creations, and a healthy wrangling over ideas and viewpoints. While there must be a definite foundation and "solid core" in the educational system, as discussed above; and while the Revolutionary Communist Party will actively and vigorously promote its viewpoint and program throughout society; there should at the same time be available not only to students but to the broader population a rich storehouse of political and philosophical, scientific, historical, artistic and other works, expressing and reflecting a diversity of viewpoints. This is an important, indeed indispensable part of enabling students, and the people broadly, to be stimulated, sustained and enriched intellectually and culturally and to pursue the truth wherever it leads with a spirit of critical thinking and scientific curiosity, and in this way to continually learn about the world and be better able to contribute to changing it in accordance with the fundamental interests of humanity.

G. Science and Scientific Endeavor.

1. The promotion and support of science and scientific endeavor in the New Socialist Republic in North America is aimed at continually increasing the storehouse of scientific knowledge, and broadly fostering the scientific spirit and method, for the benefit of humanity. One very important dimension of this is furthering the development of the socialist economy and the material basis for carrying forward the transformation of society, and the world, toward the final goal of communism and the emancipation of humanity. But the role and purpose of science cannot be reduced to that, as important and crucial as that is. Beyond that, encouraging curiosity about the natural world, in its manifold dimensions, including human society and its historical development, and fostering and applying creative and at the same time rigorous scientific means for exploring and learning about all this, is fundamental to the full flowering of human beings and to their ability to contribute to the advance to a communist world.

With this orientation, the government, particularly through the central Executive, shall support both scientific projects and pursuits which relate and can contribute more directly to the objectives and policies of the government at any given time and scientific experimentation, research and theoretical exploration which may have no direct and immediate relation to and bearing on those objectives and policies but may hold the potential, or represent the possibility, of making new breakthroughs in scientific understanding or contributing to the process through which such breakthroughs may be made, and which in any case contribute to fostering the scientific spirit and the scientific method.

2. It shall be the orientation of the government, and concrete efforts shall be made, not only to promote and foster the scientific method but to share scientific discoveries and breakthroughs, and scientific knowledge in general, with scientists (and the broader population) in other parts of the world, and to enable this to become part of the general storehouse of knowledge of humanity as a whole, to the greatest degree possible, while also paying necessary attention, where relevant, to the security concerns of the New Socialist Republic in North America and its people.

3. While providing the necessary means, conditions and atmosphere required for and conducive to scientific work, including theoretical research and exploration, efforts shall also be made not only to provide students and the people more broadly, through the educational system and in other ways, basic scientific knowledge and grounding in scientific principles and the scientific method, but also to involve growing numbers of people in scientific research and experimentation–including in projects where they are working together with and are led by full-time scientific professionals–and to draw on the vast experience and accumulated knowledge of the people in society as a valuable resource for scientific endeavor.

H. Health and Medicine.

1. The goal of the New Socialist Republic in North America with regard to health and medicine is to promote the all-around health and well-being of the people and, as one key dimension of this, to provide the people in society as a whole with access to medical care–at low cost and eventually free of cost–and to continually develop and improve this medical care. The government of this Republic also acts to ensure that the food and nutritional needs of the population are met.

Research and other work will be done to anticipate, as much as possible, and to prevent to the greatest degree possible, outbreaks of disease and epidemics, and to detect and treat such outbreaks and epidemics as quickly and effectively as possible where and when they cannot be prevented.

2. In line with this overall orientation, while due attention will be paid to the treatment of disease, including highly specialized treatment, and to medical research (and in this regard the basic

principles discussed above with regard to science and scientific endeavor will be applied), the emphasis will be placed on prevention of disease, through the promotion of healthy nutrition and exercise, as well as other means, and on early detection and treatment of disease, to the greatest degree possible.

3. In keeping with a scientific approach, as well as an internationalist orientation, research and development, and practical developments, in the field of medicine shall be shared, as fully as possible, with people in this (and related) fields in other parts of the world, and cooperation shall be promoted and effected in detecting, combatting and preventing outbreaks of disease and epidemics, as well as in the treatment of disease, and the all-around development of medical science and its practical application, throughout the world.

4. The orientation that shall be promoted, and established as the standard, for professionals and others in the field of medicine shall be to serve the people. In the treatment of disease, and in other aspects of medicine, the sensibilities, as well as the experience and knowledge, of patients, and of the people broadly, shall be taken into account and drawn on fully as a basic requirement and a basic resource in the practice of medicine and the development and application of medical science.

I. The Media.

1. In line with the socialist orientation and principles regarding the development of the economy–and with the orientation and principles set forth in this Constitution as a whole–the ownership and use of the major media in the New Socialist Republic in North America shall be in the hands of the government and under its ultimate direction, and specifically that of the Executive Council of the central government. At the same time, as discussed below, various media that are independent of the government shall not only be allowed but, to a significant degree, funded (and otherwise facilitated) by the central government, acting through the Executive Council and agencies and other instrumentalities it may establish for this purpose (see 4, below).

2. It shall be the orientation of the media directly owned and run by the government to provide the people in society with

truthful and important information and analysis regarding affairs of state, the functioning of government, and other significant developments in society and the world. In the gathering and presentation of such information and analysis by the government media, the orientation and principles that are emphasized above (in parts F and G, relating to education and science) with regard to the pursuit of the truth and the criterion of truth, shall be applied and given particular importance, as the purpose in presenting such information and analysis is to contribute in significant ways to the ability of the people to understand and act to transform society, and the world, in the interests of humanity. And, in the service of this same objective, in addition to the funding and facilitation of alternative media independent of the government, significant allowance must be made, and time and opportunity provided, for the presentation, through the government media themselves, of a diversity of viewpoints and analysis, including ones which differ from and are in opposition to those presented by the government and its representatives. All this will be in accord with, and an application of, the principle of "solid core, with a lot of elasticity."

3. In addition to the dissemination of information and analysis of current events, affairs of state and other important developments in society and the world ("news programs" and "news media") the media owned and operated under the direction of the government shall provide an increasing volume and variety of music, drama, comedy and other artistic works which will aim to be of the highest artistic quality and with a content consistent with the principles set forth in this Constitution. (See also part J, below, regarding Art and Culture.)

4. Besides the media owned and operated under the direction of the government, provision must be made and funds and other resources allocated for the establishment and operation of media which are independent of the government and which may present views and opinions that are in opposition to those put forward by the government at any given time through its media (and in other ways). For this purpose, various bodies and other agencies shall be appointed, under the ultimate direction of the central Executive Council, to review applications and grant licenses, funding and other resources, for such independent media. In the

determination of which applications shall be granted, the criterion must not be agreement with the government, but on the contrary to facilitate the promotion and dissemination of a diversity of views and opinions, with a significant representation of views and opinions that may run contrary to those of the government at any given time, including even some which may oppose not only particular policies and actions of the government but the basic principles and objectives of the New Socialist Republic in North America. In this connection, what is discussed in Article III, Section 2 concerning freedom of speech and other rights has importance as a basic guideline.

5. In addition to media which receive government funding and other resources but which operate independently of the government, there will also be, and be allowance for, many different means of communication belonging to individuals, including those connected to the internet, and various media generated through the efforts and personal resources of individuals. Besides the ways in which this can serve as a means of individual expression, of various kinds, it can also contribute to the larger atmosphere of lively and substantive exchange of and wrangling over different ideas and viewpoints. In accordance with the orientation and principles set forth here, "self-generated" media, and in general media independent of the government, may seek to raise funds and acquire resources, beyond those which may be provided by the government, so long as these funds and resources are utilized solely for the operation of these media and do not lead to, or involve, the accumulation of private capital and the employment of people as wage workers, except as might be specifically authorized through the economic plan of the state, or by an agency of the government authorized to make such a decision in the context of the overall economic plan.

6. Through funds and other resources provided by the government–not to exceed 1/2 of the value of that provided for the independent media discussed above–and through support it receives directly from its own members and others more broadly in society, the Revolutionary Communist Party may also maintain and establish media directly under its leadership, to propagate its full program and viewpoint, the principles and methods of the Party itself and their application to various spheres of

social and international relations, and to analyze current events and important developments in society and the world, and other major questions relating to politics as well as philosophy, science, art and culture and in general matters which are of importance to society and the people and the advance to communism.

7. All this is, once again, an application of the principle of "solid core, with a lot of elasticity," a key means for enabling the broad masses of people to be exposed to, and to debate and "thrash out," various ideas and viewpoints, in order to more deeply engage, come to understand, and transform the world in the interests of humanity. And, once again as well, all this must be "embraced" by the "solid core"–with the Revolutionary Communist Party as the most decisive leading element–and enabled to contribute, through many divergent paths, to the advance along a broad road toward the goal of communism.

J. Art and Culture.

1. The sphere of art and culture responds to a profound need of human beings, who indeed cannot live simply by "bread" (the basic material requirements of life) alone, and it is also an important arena in which ideological viewpoints and values are formulated, or reflected, and transmitted, and where ideological struggle takes place over opposing viewpoints and values. All this serves as the foundation and framework for the approach to art and culture in the New Socialist Republic in North America.

2. As noted previously in this Section, there will be significant attention and resources devoted to the creation, development and popularization of art and culture by the government, for which the central Executive Council shall have overall responsibility and which shall aim to be of the highest artistic quality and with a content consistent with the principles set forth in this Constitution. This shall be effected through the development and subsidy of professional artists and artistic productions–in film, theater, literature, music, painting, sculpture, and the visual and plastic arts generally, and other spheres of culture–as well as part-time and "amateur" artistic groups and productions throughout society, with support and assistance from the relevant government bodies in the various regions, including any autonomous regions (or other autonomous areas) which may be established (where art

and culture would reflect and embody important elements of the historically evolved culture of particular nationalities), localities and basic units of society and government.

3. As with the media, provision must also be made and funds and resources allocated, by the government at the central level, as well as other levels, to support art and culture which is independent of the government and may give expression to, or reflect, ideas and views which are in opposition to the policy and actions of the government at any given time, or even to the basic principles and objectives of the New Socialist Republic in North America. Here again, the discussion of freedom of speech and other rights in Article III, Section 2 is relevant. At the same time, as the sphere of art and culture has its own particularities–and specifically as one of its main features is the use of metaphor and figurative expression, and it often involves the "skewing" of reality and the presentation of things in terms and in forms which are not, and are not intended to be, literal reproductions of everyday life but are concentrations of aspects of life in a way that should be "higher than life"–it is necessary not only to make considerable allowance for, and to appreciate the importance of, experimentation and non-conformity in this sphere but also not to confuse art and culture with, and evaluate it according to the same criteria as, political agitation and advocacy per se. This is important as a general principle but also in regard to art and culture which is "oppositional" in one way or another; and this understanding should serve as another important guideline for government bodies in regard to art and culture.

4. Along with the development of and support for more professional artists and artistic works and productions–both those under the direction of government bodies created for this purpose and those which are expressly independent of the government– the government, with the central Executive Council having ultimate responsibility, should also foster, encourage, promote and support, among the people broadly, an appreciation for art and culture and involvement in artistic endeavors and creations, in line with what is discussed in point 1 above.

5. As with the media, in the sphere of art and culture independent and "amateur" theater troupes and other artistic groups

and associations may seek to raise funds and acquire resources, beyond those which may be provided by the government, so long as these funds and resources are utilized solely for their operations and do not lead to, or involve, the accumulation of private capital and the employment of people as wage-workers, except as might be specifically authorized through the economic plan of the state, or by an agency of the government authorized to make such a decision in the overall context of the economic plan.

Also, through funds and resources provided by the government–not to exceed 1/2 the value of that provided for independent art and culture–and through support it receives directly from its own members and others more broadly in society, the Revolutionary Communist Party will produce and work to popularize a variety of artistic creations which also strive to meet the needs of the people for culture with a high artistic quality while also inspiring people with the outlook and values of communism, as this has been further developed through the new synthesis brought forward by Bob Avakian.

6. In addition to the sphere of art and artistic creation, the government (with the central Executive Council having the overall responsibility, while establishing agencies and instrumentalities for this purpose and working with government at other levels) shall also promote and support sports events and activities, to provide entertainment and recreation and promote health and fitness throughout society. This shall include some professional sports teams and leagues, while at the same time emphasis is given to the participation of people broadly, and in particular the youth, in sports of many different kinds. The role of competition in sports will be recognized and given its appropriate place, but the basic and overall priority in sports will be to foster bonds of friendship, comradeship, community, cooperation and the shared experience and joy of sport, along with its contribution to health and fitness–and the promotion of internationalism, particularly in sports activities that are engaged in together with people from other countries.

7. To further provide for the recreation of the people, and to encourage their appreciation for nature and sense of awe and wonder at its many and diverse manifestations, national parks

and other areas designated for this purpose shall be established and maintained by the government: for the preservation and protection of these areas and of many different species of animals and plants, especially those which may be endangered, of crucial ecosystems and the environment as a whole, as well as for the cultural enrichment of the people.

8. In the various dimensions mentioned here, and in the sphere of art and culture as a whole, the objective of the government of the New Socialist Republic in North America is to meet the intellectual and cultural needs and serve the largest interests of the masses of people, to foster and support the all-around development of people throughout society, and to contribute to the development of people throughout the world, whose imagination, creativity, initiative, talents and abilities are inspired and unleashed to bring into being new relations among people, and a new world, in which human beings can flourish, in ways and in dimensions never before imagined, in a spirit and in bonds of cooperation, without the fetters of oppressive divisions and the selfish, narrowing, and deadening ideas and ways of thinking which spring from and reinforce such divisions.

Section 3. The Judiciary and Legal Adjudication.

1. There shall be a uniform code of law for the Republic as a whole, consisting of laws established by the central Legislature as provided for in this Constitution (see, in particular, Section 1 of this Article). The legislatures in the various regions, including autonomous regions, localities and other units of government which may be established in accordance with this Constitution, may pass laws pertaining to their particular sphere of governance, but such laws may not be in conflict with this Constitution or with laws established by the Legislature at the central level in accordance with this Constitution. If there is a conflict between laws established by the central Legislature and laws passed by other government bodies at other levels of society, the laws established by the central Legislature shall have precedence and effect, so long as they are in conformity with this Constitution. The Constitution and laws in accordance with this Constitution in the New Socialist Republic in North America shall apply to all citizens of this Republic and to all those residing within its territory.

2. Laws established at whatever level of government, and actions of the government at whatever level, may be reviewed through the judicial system, which has the authority to determine whether or not such laws and actions are in conformity with this Constitution. Citizens and residents of the New Socialist Republic in North America have the right to challenge laws, established at whatever level of government, and actions taken by the government, at whatever level. However, except in legal proceedings in which they are defendants–in which case individuals shall have the right to legal counsel, provided by the Department of Legal Defense and Assistance at the appropriate level, and the right to appeal decisions of the courts as well as the constitutionality of laws which have been applied in those particular proceedings–citizens and residents of the New Socialist Republic in North America, in making, on their own initiative, a challenge pertaining to the constitutionality of a law or government action, must present their challenge to a legal body which shall have been established in various parts of this Republic specifically to hear and rule on such challenges; and, in this particular proceeding, those presenting such a challenge will not have the right to be provided legal representation by the Department of Legal Defense and Assistance, but must proceed on their own accord. If this legal body rules in favor of the challenge, it may then be presented to the appropriate court, and in this proceeding the person (or persons) making the challenge do have the right to legal representation, provided by the appropriate branch of the Department of Legal Defense and Assistance. If the initial ruling by this legal body is against the challenge, then the challenge may not be further pursued unless it is joined by a certain percentage of the population, 18 years and older, in the relevant area, in a manner prescribed by the legislature in that area, or by the central Legislature (for example, by requiring the requisite number of valid signatures on an authorized petition). This percentage is here set at 10%; however, this may be changed through action of the appropriate legislative body, although the percentage may not be established at less than 5% nor more than 20%, except through Amendment to this Constitution (see Article VI). If the required percentage of persons do join in such a challenge, by the means prescribed, then this challenge may proceed to a hearing at the

appropriate court, and the rules and provisions relevant to such a procedure, including the right of those making the challenge to legal representation provided by the relevant branch of the Department of Legal Defense and Assistance, shall apply.

3. The highest court in the New Socialist Republic in North America is the Supreme Court. This Supreme Court shall have the ultimate review and determination as to the constitutionality of the laws and the actions of government. The exact size of the Supreme Court shall be determined by the central Legislature, but the number of justices on the Supreme Court shall be an uneven number, not to exceed 15 nor be less than 9. Rulings of the Supreme Court, to be official, must have the votes of at least a majority of its members who are sitting in judgment of the matter at the time, constituting at least 40% of the Court's total members.

In proceedings of the Supreme Court (and other legal proceedings) both Spanish and English may be utilized, with translation from the one language into the other provided simultaneously; and translation into other relevant languages shall be provided as relevant and necessary.

4. Members of the Supreme Court are nominated by the Executive Council of the central government. These nominations are subject to review and approval by the Revolutionary Communist Party, or by a body (or bodies) established by the Party for this purpose. Such nominations are also subject to review by the central Legislature, and nominees for the Supreme Court must receive the approval of a majority of that Legislature. Once chosen, members of the Supreme Court shall serve for life, or until they retire–except in cases of violation of the Constitution, or conviction for a crime, or conduct detrimental to the role of the Court, as determined through impeachment proceedings.

5. In the case of former members and functionaries of the ruling class of the imperialist United States of America, and those acting on its behalf, who are suspected of having committed war crimes and/or other crimes against humanity, special Tribunals may be established by the central Legislature–or by the central Executive Council, with the approval of a majority of the members of the central Legislature–to try such persons for these

crimes, in accordance with principles, provisions and procedures of law, and due process of law, which have been set forth in, or in any case are in conformity with, this Constitution. Those convicted–through the proceedings of such special Tribunals, or other judicial proceedings–of such war crimes and/or other crimes against humanity shall be deprived of their liberty and shall be punished in correspondence with the severity of the crime which they shall have been convicted of committing– but this shall again be in accordance with the law and with the provisions of this Constitution, and may not include cruel and unusual punishment, or other acts which are prohibited in Article III, Section 2 of this Constitution. In the case of persons convicted of war crimes and/or other crimes against humanity, as with conviction of any other crime, punishment shall apply only to those so convicted, and may not be applied to others, merely as a result of association with those convicted, including members of their family and their descendants–who may be punished for such crimes only if they themselves are convicted of these crimes through due process of law and in accordance with the provisions set forth in this Constitution.

6. As referred to in Section 2 of this Article, the central Legislature may, by a vote of at least 2/3 of its members, initiate impeachment proceedings against members of the Supreme Court. A member of the judiciary at the next level, below that of the Supreme Court, shall preside in such proceedings. Convictions in these proceedings shall require a vote of at least 3/4 of the members of the central Legislature. A member of the Supreme Court so convicted shall be removed from office. The central Legislature may also, in accordance with the same procedures and standards, impeach members of lower courts, or may delegate to a legislature at a lower level the authority to do so, with either a judge on the Supreme Court–or in any case a judge from a higher level of the judiciary than the person being impeached–presiding in such cases. In the case of impeachment of a member of the judiciary, sanctions and requirements relevant to holding public office, as well as the fact that the person impeached and convicted may also be prosecuted for violation of the law (as discussed in Section 2 of this Article), shall also apply–except that, in addition, any member of the judiciary

who has been impeached and convicted may never again serve on the judiciary, on any level, and may not have the status of legal counsel in any capacity, except in a pro se capacity (representing herself/himself) in legal proceedings in which she or he is directly and personally involved.

7. Cases involving international relations and treaties, and questions regarding the legitimacy of elections to the central Legislature and the standing of members of that Legislature, are to be heard by the Supreme Court as the first court of jurisdiction. With regard to all other matters within its overall and ultimate authority, the Supreme Court may decide to hear, or not to hear, cases appealed to it from lower courts, and instead of hearing such a case itself, the Supreme Court may refer it to a lower court.

8. The central Legislature may establish courts at lower levels, and in doing so the Legislature shall consult with the appropriate legislative body in the given area. Legislative bodies at the various levels and in the various areas may also establish additional courts and determine the scope of their jurisdiction, so long as this is within the overall framework established by the central Legislature and is in conformity with this Constitution. The central Legislature, once again in consultation with the legislatures at the relevant lower levels, shall establish the basic structure of relations between the courts at the various levels, including the channels of appeals of decisions by courts at the various levels, with the Supreme Court being the court of last appeal.

9. The basic rights of the people–citizens and residents of the New Socialist Republic in North America–when they are accused of and prosecuted for crimes, or are otherwise involved in legal proceedings, are included in Article III of this Constitution, and these rights shall be fully recognized, accorded, protected and applied in all legal proceedings.

Article II. Regions, Localities, and Basic Institutions.

Section 1. Government in Regions, Localities, and Other Areas Within the Overall Territory of the New Socialist Republic in North America.

1. As set forth in Article I, the central Legislature shall provide for the establishment of the appropriate governmental authority and administration in regions, localities, and other areas and institutions within the New Socialist Republic in North America. (This includes autonomous regions, or other autonomous areas, which may be established where there are significant populations of minority and formerly oppressed nationalities–see Section 3.)

2. Except where otherwise indicated in this Constitution, the government at these various levels shall follow the basic model as that at the central level, as set forth in Article I, with due allowance for particularities of the region, area, or institution (including especially autonomous regions, or other autonomous areas, which may be established), within the overall structure of the New Socialist Republic in North America and in accordance with this Constitution. In regions, including autonomous regions (or other autonomous areas), and in localities, which the central Legislature shall have designated as areas of governmental authority and administration, legislatures shall be elected by the same general procedures, and following the same general provisions (including those regarding eligibility to vote and to hold office) as obtain with regard to the central Legislature (with certain differences that are indicated in part 3 in this Section). Further, within the overall structure of the New Socialist Republic in North America and in accordance with this Constitution, the legislature in these areas shall in turn be responsible for and shall have the authority to elect (and to recall or impeach) an executive council and its members for these areas, in accordance with the same basic approach and procedures which obtain in the selection of the central Executive Council by the central Legislature; and on this same basis, and within the same overall structure, the executive in these areas shall have the authority to effect the adminis-

trative functions that are set forth in Section 2 of Article I of this Constitution, in the ways that are appropriate for these regional and local areas. The legislature in these areas shall also have the authority, within the overall structure of the New Socialist Republic in North America, and in cooperation with and with overall direction by the central Legislature, to establish courts with jurisdiction within these areas, in accordance with Article I, Section 3 and with this Constitution as a whole. The principle of leadership by the Revolutionary Communist Party with regard to the central Executive (as discussed in Article I, Section 2) and of review and approval by the Party of nominees for the judiciary (as discussed in Article I, Section 3) shall also apply in regard to the executive and the courts in these areas. The principle of leadership by the Party of the armed forces, militia, and other organs of public defense and security, as set forth in Article I, Section 2, shall also apply.

3. Elections to the legislature in the geographic areas which are the subject of this Article shall be apportioned as follows (with an additional criterion for legislatures in autonomous regions and areas which may be established, as set forth in Section 3):

i. 1/3 of the total seats shall be determined through votes cast by the leadership bodies of the basic units of society in these areas–workplaces, neighborhoods, educational institutions, and other institutions designated by the legislature at the central level and/or the area legislature (see Section 2 in this Article).

ii. 1/3 of the total seats shall be determined through votes cast through direct popular election, with voting by districts (or similar geographical designations), established for the purpose of such election by the legislature for the area. Everyone eligible to vote and to hold office may stand for election in this process.

iii. 1/3 of the total seats shall be determined through votes cast by direct popular election (as in point ii above, including the same eligibility requirements), with the difference that those standing for election in this 1/3 apportionment will have been recommended by a nominating council established and led by the Revolutionary Communist Party (as with elections to the central Legislature, it shall be the general orientation of this council, and of the Party in establishing and leading it, that wherever and whenever feasible more than one group of candidates shall be nominated and that those nominated shall reflect a diversity of views, within the overall framework of the principles and objectives set forth in the Preamble and elsewhere in this Constitution).

4. Members of these legislatures shall serve for 4 years. The basic principles and provisions regarding impeachment of members of the central Legislature, as well as of the executive and the judiciary, shall apply on these levels as well, again with due allowance for the particularities of the region or area.

Section 2. Basic Institutions.

1. Governing and leadership bodies shall be established in all the basic institutions of society, as established by the central Legislature and/or the legislature at other levels. These governing and leadership bodies shall exercise both decision-making and executive functions and shall work in close coordination and cooperation with those they lead.

2. These leadership bodies shall be elected as follows:

i. 1/2 shall be chosen by direct popular vote from among candidates recommended by the Revolutionary Communist Party (or by a body appointed by the Party for this purpose). Here again, the principles discussed above, concerning the orientation and approach in regard to the nomination of such candidates, shall be applied.

ii. 1/2 shall be chosen by direct popular vote in which all those eligible to vote in such an election, and to hold office, may stand for election.

iii. Those who stand for election–in accordance with points i and ii above–must reside or work in, or regularly attend or regularly take part in, the particular institution (according to its specific nature) and must be 18 years of age or older, with the exception that in educational (and other) institutions where there are a significant number of persons under the age of 18, provision should be made (by the leadership body in question) for the selection and participation of a certain percentage of such persons in this leadership body, provided that this amounts to less than 1/3 of the leadership body.

3. These leadership bodies shall serve for 2 years.

4. These leadership bodies shall, through meetings and assemblies and in other ways, report on their work and hold discussions of this work–and other matters of concern not only regarding the particular institution but the larger society and world–with those regularly involved in these institutions. In this and other ways, these leadership bodies and the members of these bodies should strive to build close relations with, to listen to the opinions and criticisms of, and to learn from at the same time as leading the people who are the foundation of these basic institutions, and of the society as a whole. This fundamental principle and approach should be applied by leadership in general, at all levels of society and government.

5. The leadership bodies of these basic institutions may be recalled by a vote of at least 2/3 of all those who are eligible to vote in elections for these leadership bodies (with voting in regard to such recall in accordance with what is set forth in points 2,i and 2,ii above).

Section 3. Minority and Formerly Oppressed Nationalities.

1. In light of the egregious crimes, oppression and injustice perpetrated by the former ruling class and government of the United States of America against various minority nationalities, to give expression to the voluntary union and growing unity of the various peoples within the New Socialist Republic in North America, and to give the most powerful effect to the principles and objectives set forth in this Constitution, discrimination against minority nationalities, in every sphere of society, including segregation in housing, education and other areas, shall be outlawed and prohibited, and concrete measures and steps shall be adopted and carried out, by the government at the central and other levels, to overcome the effects of discrimination and segregation, and the whole legacy of oppression, to which these peoples have been subjected.

As one important dimension of this, in regions (or other areas) of significant population concentration of minority nationalities which were oppressed within the borders of the former imperialist USA, there shall be the right of the people of those nationalities to autonomy, in the form of self-government within the overall territory, framework and structure of the New Socialist Republic in North America and its unified socialist economy, system of law, armed forces, and conduct of foreign relations.

The decisions regarding the establishment (or not) of various autonomous regions shall be made through elections–to be held under the auspices of a commission established by the central Legislature, consulting with people from among various and diverse sections of the nationalities concerned–within one year after the founding of the New Socialist Republic in North America. In such elections, only members of the particular nationality in question who are eligible to vote in elections in this Republic shall vote. If a majority of those taking part in such an election vote in favor of establishing an autonomous region, that autonomous region shall be established, within one year after such an election, in accordance with what is set forth in this Constitution. In the event that a majority vote against establishing such an autonomous region, a vote on this question may be held again in 5 years, in accordance with the provisions set forth here. Also, if less than a majority but more than 1/3 of those taking part in an election concerning an autonomous region vote in favor of establishing such an autonomous region, the central Legislature may, by a vote of at least 2/3 of its members, establish such a region. In keeping with the orientation, principles and objectives set forth in this Section, and throughout this Constitution, where such autonomous regions are established they provide an opportunity for people of the nationality concerned to live in areas of significant concentration of that nationality, if they so choose, but they shall not be required to live in such areas, and once again it shall be the orientation, policy, and active purpose of the government, at all levels, to prohibit and work to overcome the effects of discrimination and segregation that have been directed against these nationalities, and generally to promote integration and unity among the various nationalities throughout society, on the basis of equality.

2. The governments in any autonomous regions that are established shall be structured and chosen in accordance with the basic principles and procedures that obtain with regard to the central government and governments in various other areas within the

overall New Socialist Republic in North America, while these autonomous region governments will also have the right to create additional institutional structures and procedures that may be necessary for the realization and functioning of autonomy, particularly as regards the language and culture of the nationalities concerned, so long as this is in accordance with the Constitution and laws of the New Socialist Republic in North America. Where there may be a conflict between a law or policy in an autonomous region and the laws and policies of the central government, those of the central government shall, so long as they are in accordance with this Constitution, have precedence and effect; but other than in such circumstances, wide scope should be given to governments in autonomous regions with regard to policy and law, particularly as that applies to language and culture.

3. Elections to the legislature–and in turn the role of the legislature in relation to the executive and courts–in autonomous regions shall be carried out as set forth in this Constitution, including in particular Section 2 of this Article, with the added criterion that, in these autonomous regions, attention must be paid to ensuring that a majority, or at least a plurality, of representatives in the legislature of such a region consists of people of the nationality for which the region was primarily established.

4. The legislature in any autonomous region may, by a simple majority vote of its members, initiate a procedure by which the eligible voters in that autonomous region will vote on whether to continue that region as an autonomous entity, within the overall New Socialist Republic in North America, or to abolish that region and integrate its governmental structures into those of the larger Republic as a whole. In such an election, the decision shall be made by a simple majority vote.

5. Looking beyond the first elections–to be held within one year after the founding of the New Socialist Republic in North America–with regard to the establishment (or not) of autonomous regions, procedures shall also be established by the central Legislature which shall provide for the possibility of the creation of autonomous regions in the future, in accordance with what is set forth in this Section, and in this Constitution as a whole. The central Legislature, in consultation with any relevant autonomous

region legislature, shall also provide the means and procedures for the possible establishment of autonomy in areas, smaller than regions, in which there is a significant concentration of people of a formerly oppressed nationality. Such autonomous areas as may be established shall be governed in accordance with the basic principles and provisions set forth in this Section and elsewhere in this Constitution, while at the same time taking into account the particular situation and needs of the people in such autonomous areas.

6. Policies with Regard to Particular Nationalities, and Immigrants.

A. African-Americans.

1. If an African-American autonomous region is established, in accordance with what is set forth above in this Section, and in this Constitution overall, the territory of this autonomous region shall be within what was the southern part of the former imperialist United States of America–the area where the enslavement and then the continuing oppression of Black people within that imperialist state had its most concentrated historical foundation and roots and where large numbers of Black people still lived at the time of the revolution which put an end to that imperialist state and brought into being the New Socialist Republic in North America.

2. Further, there shall be the right of African-Americans to self-determination, up to and including the right to secede from the New Socialist Republic in North America and to form a separate country, with its own independent government, in the same general territory where the autonomous African-American region would be established within the New Socialist Republic in North America. If called for by a vote of a least 2/3 of the members of the legislature of the African-American autonomous region, this right to secede and form a separate country will be put to a vote and decided by such a vote, in which African-Americans who reside in the overall territory of the New Socialist Republic in North America, and who are eligible to vote in elections in this Republic, shall be the only people eligible to vote. If, as a result of the vote on the question of autonomy (as set forth above in this Section), an African-American autonomous region has not been established, then a referendum on African-American secession

may be called for by the central Legislature, through a vote of 2/3 or more of its members–and the central Legislature will be required to vote on whether to call for such a referendum if it is requested to do so by at least 1/3 of its members.

In the event of such a referendum on secession, the procedures relating to it shall be under the supervision of a joint commission established by the central Legislature and the legislature of the African-American autonomous region (if such an autonomous region has been established) and consisting of an equal number of members appointed by each of these two legislatures. If, as a result of the vote on the question of autonomy, an African-American autonomous region has not been established, then the commission to oversee the referendum on secession shall be appointed by the central Legislature, consulting with people from among various and diverse sections of the African-American population. The composition of this commission shall be at least 50% African-American, and this commission, once selected, shall be independent and shall act independently of the central Legislature. The procedures regarding the referendum on secession must include equal access to the government media, within the African-American autonomous region (if such an autonomous region exists) and throughout the New Socialist Republic in North America, for representatives of both sides in this referendum.

As a decision to secede is a momentous one, and one not easily reversed–and therefore ample time and opportunity should be provided for serious reflection, discussion, deliberation and consideration concerning this matter–a vote regarding such secession would be held as follows. A first referendum would be held one year after this referendum has been called for, through procedures indicated above. Those eligible to vote on this referendum (as stipulated here) would vote in favor either of remaining within the New Socialist Republic in North America or of seceding from it. If 50% or more of those voting on this referendum declared in favor of secession, then a second referendum would be held one year after that, with the same eligibility standards for voting and the same basic procedures. In that second referendum, if once again 50% or more of those voting declared in favor of secession, then this secession would be effected. In that event, the government of the New Socialist Republic in North America would, to the best of its ability under the circumstances and in accordance with the principles and objectives set forth in this Constitution, work to establish relations with the new country established as a result of this secession and to encourage, and as far as possible support and assist, that new country in taking the road of socialism and contributing to the international revolutionary struggle toward the final goal of a communist world. Notwithstanding the difficulty and complications that might be involved, the New Socialist Republic in North America would also remain open to, and would welcome, a reunion, in one state, with the country established through such secession, provided this were effected in accordance with the principles and objectives set forth in this Constitution.

3. In accordance with the principles and provisions set forth above in this Section, and in this Constitution overall, autonomous areas may be established and function in cities and other areas within the New Socialist Republic in North America which have significant concentrations of African-Americans.

B. Mexican-Americans.

1. What was the southwest region of the former United States of America was seized by that country—as part of the expansion of the slave system, and other relations of exploitation and oppression—through armed conquest, including war against Mexico, in the 19th century. Given this history, and after that a long period marked by the domination and exploitation of Mexico and its people by the imperialist United States of America, large numbers of people of Mexican origin and descent have for many generations lived in this region, with their ranks continually expanded by new immigrants forced to leave Mexico because of the continuing effects of domination and exploitation by the USA. They were joined by growing numbers of people from other countries in Latin America which were also subjected to the same kind of domination and depredation at the hands of the imperialist USA. In view of this, and as an expression of proletarian internationalism and of the other basic principles and objectives set forth in this Constitution, the following shall be the orientation and policies of the New Socialist Republic in North America with regard to this region.

2. Relations with Mexico, and policy with regard to the former southwest region of the imperialist USA, shall, from the time of the founding and in the first few years of the New Socialist Republic in North America, take into account the nature of the society and government–and the level and character of revolutionary struggle–in Mexico, as well as the actual extent of territory which has been liberated through the revolution which led to the defeat and dismantling of the imperialist state of the USA and the founding of the New Socialist Republic in North America. At the same time, the necessary consideration shall be given to the situation in the world as a whole, in determining how to proceed with regard to this region. In this overall context, and also taking into account the sentiments and aspirations of the people in the region, in particular those of Mexican origin and descent, the question of whether to return at least parts of this region to Mexico, and/or whether there should be established, within parts of this region, a country that is separate from both Mexico and the New Socialist Republic in North America, shall be taken up by the government of the New Socialist Republic in North America.

3. In any case, within this region–or the part of it that remains within the New Socialist Republic in North America–the right of autonomy of Mexican-Americans shall be recognized and approached in accordance with the principles and objectives set forth in this Article and in this Constitution as a whole.

4. In accordance with the principles and provisions set forth above in this Section, and in this Constitution overall, autonomous areas may be established and function in cities and other areas within the New Socialist Republic in North America which have significant concentrations of Mexican-Americans.

C. Native Americans.

1. The conquest, domination, plunder and life-stealing exploitation carried out by European colonialism in the Americas–including by the European settlers who founded the United States of America and expanded its reach on the North American continent through force and violence, as well as deception and other means–had a massive genocidal impact, decimating and devastating the populations of the first inhabitants of the Americas. As the boundaries of the USA were continuously expanded through

conquest–and huge numbers of Native Americans were killed or died off due to this armed expansionism and the destruction of their way of life, the spread of diseases common among Europeans for which the Native Americans had no immunity, and other factors–most of the Native Americans who survived were forced onto reservations that were encircled and controlled by the forces of the imperialist state.

2. The defeat of this imperialist state has opened the way to overcoming the effects and legacy of this terrible history. As one key expression of the importance it attaches to this, the New Socialist Republic in North America shall ensure that the right of autonomy of Native American peoples within this Republic is upheld; and, beyond that, wherever autonomous regions of Native Americans may be established, in the general vicinity of the historical homelands of the various native peoples, the central government will also act to ensure that these autonomous regions not only have the necessary territories but also the resources that will enable a real flourishing of these peoples, within the overall framework of the New Socialist Republic in North America. The central government of the New Socialist Republic in North America will provide special assistance and support to any Native American autonomous regions, on the basis of the principles and objectives set forth in this Constitution.

3. This special assistance and support shall be especially important with regard to Native American autonomous regions, but also with regard to concentrations of Native Americans in urban areas and other parts of this Republic–where autonomous Native American areas may also be set up–and with regard to the Native American population as a whole.

Such special assistance and support will also be of great importance, and shall be extended, to all the formerly oppressed peoples, and any autonomous regions and areas of these peoples, within the New Socialist Republic in North America.

D. With regard to other minority nationalities within the New Socialist Republic in North America, the basic orientation and policies to outlaw and prohibit, and to overcome the effects of, discrimination and segregation shall be applied. The central government may, as it deems necessary, provide the means by which autonomous areas could be established in localities where there are significant numbers of these minority nationalities, applying the basic principles that obtain with regard to autonomy within the larger Republic.

E. The Nation of Puerto Rico and Puerto Ricans Within the New Socialist Republic in North America.

1. Puerto Rico and its people were subjected to brutal conquest and domination–first by the Spanish Conquistadors and then by U.S. imperialism, forcibly seizing Puerto Rico at the end of the 19th century–with devastating and even genocidal consequences for the first inhabitants of the island and then the enslaving exploitation of others. Through this process, however, a Puerto Rican nation was forged on that island territory, even as Puerto Rico itself continued to be held as a colonial possession of the imperialist United States of America. As a result of the revolution which brought into being the New Socialist Republic in North America, the hold of U.S. imperialism over Puerto Rico has been broken, and the New Socialist Republic in North America recognizes the independence and right of self-determination of the nation of Puerto Rico. At the same time, the New Socialist Republic in North America works to develop relations with the nation of Puerto Rico on the basis of the internationalist orientation and other principles and objectives set forth in this Constitution, and remains open to the possibility of a union with the nation of Puerto Rico, in a larger socialist state, on this basis.

2. With regard to Puerto Ricans within the territory of the New Socialist Republic in North America, the principles and policies that apply to minority nationalities which were oppressed and discriminated against in the imperialist USA shall be applied, including the right to the establishment of autonomous areas in cities and other places where there are significant numbers of Puerto Ricans.

F. Hawai'i, and Other Formerly Occupied Territories.

1. Hawai'i, too, was seized from the indigenous people there by an expanding U.S. imperialism through force as well as deception. In over 100 years of domination, the USA incorporated Hawai'i into its imperialist state while maintaining it as a major

military basing area, continually suppressing the native people and degrading aspects of their culture, and the natural beauty and wonder of Hawai'i, into capitalist commodities. As a result, the indigenous people became a minority of the population on the Hawai'ian islands while, because of these same factors–and in particular the large presence of the imperialist military in Hawai'i–there has been a close interconnection between the revolutionary struggle in Hawai'i and in the continental U.S. against the same imperialist system. With the victory of the revolution leading to the defeat and dismantling of the imperialist state of the USA, the New Socialist Republic in North America recognizes and supports the right of the indigenous people of Hawai'i to self-rule and to play a decisive role in determining the direction of the society in Hawai'i, while at the same time encouraging and supporting those forces which are striving to take the road of socialism in Hawai'i and to develop the closest possible unity with the New Socialist Republic in North America, including the possibility of being part of this Republic, on the basis of the principles set forth in this Constitution.

2. The same basic orientation and approach shall be applied to other areas, outside of North America, which were seized by the imperialist USA and maintained, under its domination, as "territories" of its empire.

G. Where contradictions may arise regarding the territories of autonomous regions and areas of different nationalities that are established within the New Socialist Republic in North America, these contradictions shall be resolved through consultation involving the central government and the nationalities affected, in accordance with the basic principles set forth in this Constitution.

H. Immigrants, Citizenship and Asylum.

1. Throughout its history and its development into an imperialist power, the United States of America depended on the exploitation, often in extreme conditions, of generations of immigrants, numbering in the many millions, who were driven to the USA as a result of oppression, poverty, war and upheaval. These immigrants–including those from Europe who came to the USA during the latter part of the 19th and the first part of the 20th century, or at least several generations of them–were also subjected to discrimination

and demeaning treatment, although after a period of time many of these immigrant groups were integrated into the larger "white European" population in the USA and, on the basis of expansion and conquest by U.S. imperialism, and the spoils acquired in this way, many were able to rise from the ranks of the working class and poorer sections of the population and become a part of the "American middle class," with a more or less privileged position in relation to especially the lower and more exploited sections of the proletariat and the masses of Black and Latino people and others concentrated, and forcibly contained, within the decaying and repressive confines of the inner cities of late imperial America. At the same time, and in a heightening way through the end of the 20th and the first part of the 21st century, as a result of the domination and plunder carried out by U.S. imperialism throughout most of the Third World in particular, and the devastation and massive dislocation that resulted from and accompanied this, great numbers of immigrants from Mexico and elsewhere in Latin America, as well as other parts of the Third World, were driven to the U.S., many of whom were not able to secure legal entry and consequently were forced to live in the shadows and remain vulnerable to extreme exploitation as well as to discrimination and to violence and terror carried out by the state and by mobs encouraged by reactionary policies, actions and statements of the government and government officials. And the ruling forces of the imperialist USA seized on this situation to further tighten control over, and unleash more terror against, these immigrants and to subject many of them to even more extreme exploitation, while whipping up a xenophobic and fascist anti-immigrant atmosphere.

The defeat and dismantling of the imperialist USA and its machinery of violent destruction and repression has radically changed this situation. In this revolutionary struggle, and its victory, large numbers of immigrants, as well as masses of Black people and other oppressed nationalities within the former imperialist USA, played a crucial role, and they can and must continue to play a vital part in the continuing transformation of society, and the world as a whole, as part of the backbone of the New Socialist Republic in North America.

2. At the time of the establishment of the New Socialist Republic in North America, all those residing within the territory of this

Republic–with the exception of those who played a leading role in opposing the revolution which brought about the establishment of this Republic, and/or who may have been found guilty of war crimes and/or other crimes against humanity–shall have been accorded citizenship in this Republic, with the rights and responsibilities of citizens, in accordance with this Constitution. And, from that time forward, all those born within the territory of the New Socialist Republic in North America, as well as all those, wherever they are born, who have at least one parent who is a citizen of this Republic, shall be citizens of this Republic.

3. The orientation of the New Socialist Republic in North America is to welcome immigrants from all over the world who have a sincere desire to contribute to the goals and objectives of this Republic, as set forth in this Constitution and in laws and policies which are established and enacted in accordance with this Constitution. From the time of the establishment of the New Socialist Republic in North America, anyone residing outside of the territory of this Republic who wishes to enter its territory, and any such person wishing to become a citizen, or a permanent resident, of this Republic, must follow the relevant laws and procedures which have been established on the basis of this Constitution. Anyone who applies for asylum in this Republic and, through the relevant procedures that have been established for this purpose, is found to have been persecuted, or to have a well-founded fear of persecution, on account of having taken part in just struggles against imperialist and reactionary states or other reactionary forces, or on account of scientific, artistic, or other pursuits which have brought them into conflict with reactionary powers and institutions, shall be afforded asylum in the New Socialist Republic in North America, so long as they pledge to act in compliance with the Constitution of this Republic, and do act accordingly. Provided that they do not engage in any serious violation of the laws of this Republic, people granted asylum have the right to remain within the territory of this Republic for as long as they choose to do so, and shall be accorded the same rights as citizens, with the exception that, so long as they have not become citizens, they may not vote in elections or be elected or appointed to public office. They shall have the right, after a certain period, determined by law, to become citizens of this Republic, with the

same rights and responsibilities as all other citizens. The citizenship process, as well as review of the asylum status of all those granted asylum, shall be carried out in accordance with the laws and procedures established for these purposes.

4. Anyone who is discovered to have entered the territory of this Republic without following the relevant laws and procedures, shall be detained and provided with a timely hearing, conducted by the government institution with the relevant responsibility, to determine the reasons for their presence within this Republic. In connection with this process, such persons may apply for asylum or seek residency on some other basis, and these requests will be considered in the light of the basic orientation and principles set forth here. If, however, evidence emerges which would indicate that the person, or persons, in question have entered the territory of this Republic not only by means that are in violation of its laws, but also with the intent to further violate the law in an effort to carry out sabotage or otherwise do harm to this Republic and its people, then criminal proceedings shall be instituted against such a person, or persons, in accordance with laws and legal procedures established on the basis of this Constitution.

Article III. Rights of the People and the Struggle to Uproot All Exploitation and Oppression.

Section 1. The Basic Right of the People, the Purpose and Role of the Government, and Contradictions Between the People and the Government, in the New Socialist Republic in North America.

1. The most basic right of the proletariat, together with the broad masses of people, in the New Socialist Republic in North America is to be enabled to have the fundamentally decisive role in determining the direction of society, and to join in struggle with others throughout the world, in order to finally abolish relations of exploitation and oppression; and to bring into being, and increasingly play the determining role in regard to, government which will be an instrument toward those ends.

2. The purpose of the government of the New Socialist Republic in North America is to act in accordance with the principles and objectives set forth in this Constitution, in order to meet the basic needs and above all to serve the most fundamental and largest interests of the proletariat, together with the broad masses of people, within this Republic and ultimately in the world as a whole, with the aim of contributing as much as possible to the emancipation of all humanity, through the advance to communism.

At the same time, owing to remaining and still deep-seated contradictions, within this Republic and in the world overall–including contradictions between this Republic and imperialist and reactionary states, as well as contradictions within the economic (production) relations and the social relations, and the reflections of all this in the political, ideological and cultural spheres in this society itself–there are, and for some time will continue to be, contradictions between the people and the government in this Republic, and there is the possibility for the government, or particular agencies or persons with authority within the government, to act in conflict with the purpose and rightful role of this government. For these reasons, provisions must be made, and adhered to, which shall afford people in this Republic protection against government misconduct and abuse. And essential guidelines must be clearly set down by which the policy and actions of the government can be evaluated, with regard to particular rights, and above all the most basic right of the people in this Republic.

Section 2. Legal and Civil Rights and Liberties.

1. In keeping with what is set forth in this Constitution as a whole, and specifically in the above Section of this Article, the orientation of the government, and that promoted in society overall, must be to not only allow but to value dissent, as well as political, philosophical and in general intellectual and cultural ferment and diversity, and to promote and foster an atmosphere in which all this can flourish. This shall find expression and be embodied in government policy and action, as well as in the law, including that part of law and policy specifically intended to protect the legal and civil rights and liberties of the people in this Republic.

In the New Socialist Republic in North America, the capitalist system has been overthrown and a socialist economic system–

in which the right to employment and income is guaranteed–is being constructed, and there is ongoing transformation not only of the economy but of the society as a whole, including in the cultural and ideological realm, with a radically new morality being brought forward, in keeping with the goal of uprooting exploitation and oppression: for these reasons, "common crime" has ceased to be a major social problem, as it was in the former imperialist USA. But it has not yet been possible to eliminate all such crime, and more fundamentally, for the reasons touched on above in this Article, there remain contradictions between the people and the government. So long as that is the case, there is the prospect of political crimes against this Republic and its government, but also the possibility of ill-founded and wrongful arrest and prosecution of people for allegedly committing both political as well as "common" crimes. It is for this reason that, as set forth in Article I, Section 2, a Department of Legal Defense and Assistance shall be established, at the central level and at the various other levels of governmental and administrative responsibility, and this Department, while funded by the government, shall in every other way be independent of and operate independently of the government, in representing citizens and residents of the New Socialist Republic in North America when they are accused of crimes, as well as in other legal proceedings in which they confront the government in an adversarial position and have a right to legal representation.

2. No person in the New Socialist Republic in North America shall be deprived of the rights set forth in this Constitution, except through due process of law.

Through the course of and as a result of the revolutionary struggle which led to the defeat and dismantling of the former imperialist United States of America, and which has brought into being the New Socialist Republic in North America, members and functionaries of the former imperialist ruling class and its government and state apparatus–and in particular those who had been responsible for the most egregious crimes against the people and against humanity–will have been duly punished, in accordance with the necessities and requirements of that revolutionary struggle and the fundamental principles that guided and governed it.

Also, with the advance of that revolutionary struggle, as territory was increasingly wrenched from the control of the imperialists, growing numbers of people who had been imprisoned under the rule of those imperialists came under the jurisdiction of the advancing revolutionary forces. In this situation, the policy of the revolutionary forces with regard to these prisoners was to immediately abolish the inhumane conditions to which they had been subjected, and to begin a process through which they could learn more fully about the world and the struggle to transform it, and could have the best basis to transform their own world outlook and become conscious partisans of the revolutionary cause. To the degree possible, depending on the strength of the revolutionary forces and the overall situation, those who had been incarcerated in the dungeons of the imperialists, and who had in fact become partisan to the revolution, were provided with means to become actively involved in this revolution, in accordance with its basic principles.

Since the establishment of the New Socialist Republic in North America, the orientation and policy of the government of this Republic has been to enable as many as possible of those imprisoned under the old imperialist system to not only be freed from prison and integrated into the new society but to contribute in many ways to the continuing revolution, and to further transform themselves in the process. To this end, special bodies were set up to review, as quickly as possible, the cases and the situations of all those who had been incarcerated under the old imperialist system and who remained imprisoned at the time of the founding of the New Socialist Republic in North America. This resulted in release from prison, within a relatively short period, for the great majority—with the exception of those who had committed truly egregious offenses in the past and who showed no genuine signs that they were able, willing and determined to avail themselves of the chance, with the triumph of the revolution and the founding of the new revolutionary society, to radically transform themselves, and contribute to transforming the larger world, with the goal of uprooting relations of domination, oppression, and exploitation and the ways of thinking that go along with all that. Among the great majority who were released, this generally involved a transition period in which supervision by the relevant authority was combined with active support and assistance, including education, both practical and political–with the length and specific character of this transition process determined in accordance with the particular history and needs of the different individuals. Political education and ideological struggle has also been carried out in the society overall, to contribute to an atmosphere in which people broadly would understand the actual reasons and causes for crime in the old society and the importance of creating the conditions and atmosphere in which those who had been incarcerated as a result of criminal activity in that old society could be welcomed and supported in devoting their energies, creativity, initiative, and determination to building the new revolutionary society and carrying forward the revolutionary process in these radically new conditions. The result has been that, in addition to a significant number of people who were discovered to have been wrongfully prosecuted and imprisoned under the old system, and were therefore immediately released and provided with the means to become actively involved in the new society and its revolutionary transformation, literally millions of men and women–who had been denied a decent life in the old society; who had become involved in criminal activity, owing to their often desperate conditions and in many cases to the influence of the prevailing outlook and values in that old society, which constantly encouraged and in many ways rewarded advancing one's interests at the expense of and through the domination of others; and who had been written off as subhuman, and confined in subhuman conditions, by the guardians and enforcers of the old order–have regained and reasserted their humanity through active involvement in the new, revolutionary society, with many of them having joined the front ranks of revolution to remake the whole world in the interests of humanity.

This New Socialist Republic in North America having been established, its Constitution adopted and in effect, and its government at various levels operating in accordance with this Constitution: from that time forward, only as a matter of law, and through due process of law, may people be imprisoned or otherwise deprived of rights and liberties. This shall apply to those– including former members and functionaries of the ruling class of the imperialist USA and its state and government apparatus–

who are within the jurisdiction of this Republic and who may be accused of having in the past committed, or may in the future be accused of committing, war crimes and crimes against humanity: whether tried in special Tribunals established to preside in cases of war crimes and other crimes against humanity (as set forth in Article I, Section 3) or in other judicial proceedings, all those accused of crimes shall be treated in accordance with the laws, and due process of law.

3. The following shall apply with regard to the New Socialist Republic in North America and those residing within its territory:

A. Freedom of speech, of assembly and association, and of dissent and protest shall not be restricted, except in cases of violation of the law and through due process of law.

Expression of opposition to this Republic and its Constitution and government–including advocacy in favor of abolishing this Republic and replacing it with another kind of society and form of government–shall not be prohibited, and on the contrary shall be permitted and protected, except as this shall involve the commission, or an active conspiracy to commit, or the direct and immediate advocacy of, violent acts, which are not in self-defense, against the government or members of the government, or others residing in this Republic, or other actions which violate the law (but, once again, expression of opposition to this Republic and its government, or mere advocacy in favor of replacing this with another form of society and government, may not be declared and treated as a violation of the law).

B. The right to strike. In the event of a strike, particularly one involving state-owned sections of the economy, the government shall work to effect a resolution which will best meet the needs and requirements of the people involved, on the basis of and in accordance with the needs of society and the people overall and the principles and objectives set forth in this Constitution. In any event, no violent means may be used to end a strike and suppress those on strike, except as may be necessary in cases of violation of the law; and in general, in working to resolve such situations, means of persuasion and appeals to the largest interests of the proletariat and masses of people shall be fundamentally relied upon.

C. The right to travel. Citizens and lawful residents of the New Socialist Republic in North America are free to travel anywhere within the territory of this Republic, and may not be restricted in such travel, by action of any agency of the government, at any level, except in accordance with the law and due process of law (but laws may not be passed whose essential or primary purpose is to restrict travel within this Republic, except insofar as a violation of some other law is involved). With regard to travel from this Republic to other countries and parts of the world–and return to this Republic–this shall not be prohibited or interfered with, except in accordance with laws and legitimate security concerns which shall be adopted and acted upon by agencies of the government on the basis of, and in conformity with, this Constitution. Aside from what is set forth in the provisions in this Constitution concerning immigration into and asylum and residency in the New Socialist Republic in North America, with regard to people from other countries and parts of the world who wish to enter and remain for a certain period within this Republic, for one or another purpose, it shall be the general orientation of the government of this Republic to welcome and allow such travel, so long, again, as this shall be in conformity with the law and legitimate security concerns. Reasonable measures, which are in accord with these principles, shall be adopted by the government and its agencies to regulate travel from and into this Republic.

D. Individuals 18 years or older may own firearms for personal use, so long as this is in conformity with regulations that are established in this regard, and other laws that are established, in accordance with this Constitution. The use by others, less than 18 years, of firearms must be under the supervision of someone 18 years or older and in conformity with what is set forth here, and elsewhere in this Constitution.

E. No one shall be subjected to denial or abridgement of rights or liberty, or to discrimination, on the basis of nationality, gender, sexual orientation, or religious or other belief.

F. The right to religious belief and religious practice shall not be denied or abridged, except in the case of violation of the law and through due process of law. At the same time, religion and religious practice may not be used to carry out exploitation and to accumulate private capital, in violation of the law, or to engage in violation of the law in some other way; nor may religious persons, groups, or institutions be granted rights or privileges which do not apply to the people in this Republic in general.

The right not to practice religion or to hold religious beliefs, and to propagate atheism, shall also be upheld.

The separation of religion and the state shall be upheld and applied: No government body, and no representative of the government, may advocate or propagate and promote religion, nor on the other hand suppress or restrict religious belief and practice, except in accordance with provisions here and elsewhere in this Constitution and laws in conformity with this Constitution. No functions of the state or of the law may be performed in the name of religion or by persons or institutions invoking religious authority.

The principles and functioning of the government in various spheres, including the educational system in particular–and its promotion of the scientific method and approach, a spirit of critical and rational thinking, the pursuit of the truth and correspondence with objective reality as the criterion of truth– shall be carried out in accordance with what is set forth in this Constitution, and this may not be interfered with on the basis of religious belief or practice or through claims of exception based in religious belief or practice. In the educational system, religious beliefs and practices should be analyzed and discussed in terms of their social and cultural content and role, as well as their historical roots and development–in the same way, and in accordance with the same approach and standards, as should be applied with regard to all other social and historical phenomena.

Particularly with regard to formerly oppressed nationalities, insofar as aspects of religious belief and practice are interwoven with the historically evolved culture of the people, the orientation and approach of the government shall be to seek to separate out from religious belief and practice those aspects of the people's culture which are in accord with the basic interests of the people and can contribute to enriching the lives of not only the people of the particular nationality but the people more generally, and which should be preserved and developed in line with what is set forth in this Constitution, while maintaining the separation of religion and the state.

In addition to the role of the government with regard to education, science and other spheres, the Revolutionary Communist Party will vigorously propagate and advocate for the communist worldview, with its foundation in dialectical and historical materialism, and, as an important part of this, will actively and vigorously promote atheism and engage in lively debate with advocates of religious and other viewpoints which are in opposition to the communist worldview.

G. With regard to the law, legal proceedings, and punishment in accordance with the law, the following shall apply:

i. Freedom from arbitrary and unreasonable stops and searches –and from other infringements of basic rights and liberties, by organs of public security or other government institutions, except on the basis of law and due process of law.

ii. The prevention of unlawful imprisonment and punishment, including through the right of <u>habeas corpus</u>, that is, the right of persons accused and arrested to be presented before and to have a hearing before a court–on the basis of the law and due process of law–with regard to accusations and charges against them, in a timely manner (within 48 hours after detention). This right, however, may be suspended, or its application adjusted, in circumstances of extraordinary emergency (as discussed in H, below).

iii. No one shall be subjected to "double jeopardy" with regard to a crime for which they are accused and prosecuted–that is, after being tried and acquitted no one may be tried again for the same crime. Nor shall there be any "ex post facto" application of the law: no one may be arrested or prosecuted for an act which was not against the law in the New Socialist Republic in North America at the time the act was committed but may then have been subsequently prohibited by law.

iv. The central Legislature–and the legislatures at other levels, within the overall framework of the Constitution and laws of this Republic–may, within the spheres of their authority and responsibility, establish laws as to the "statute of limitations" (the time after which someone may no longer be prosecuted) with regard to various violations of the law.

v. Everyone accused of a crime and arrested has the right to legal representation, provided by the appropriate branch or arm of the Department of Legal Defense and Assistance, established and funded by the government but acting independently of the government on behalf of those it represents (see Article I, Sections 2 and 3). Defendants in such cases may also represent themselves, with or without the assistance of legal counsel, unless it is determined, in a hearing in open court, that they are unable to adequately provide for their own defense, in which case the assistance of legal counsel shall be mandatory. Those accused and arrested must be informed, immediately upon their arrest, of the right to legal counsel and the right to remain silent. If they are not immediately informed of these rights, or if these rights are in some other way violated by those detaining them, then any evidence against them acquired as a result of such violation may not be used against them.

vi. Along with the right of <u>habeas corpus</u> and other measures to prevent unlawful detention and denial of rights and liberty, defendants in criminal cases have the right to a timely trial and to reasonable bail before trial, as determined in a legal hearing presided over by a judge. Such a bail hearing must be held in a timely manner after arrest. The basic orientation with regard to bail shall be consistent with "the presumption of innocence." The approach to bail shall take into account remaining differences in income, and related factors, with regard to different defendants, so that such factors do not result in some defendants being effectively denied bail, when they otherwise have a right to it. While provision should be made to ensure the appearance of the defendant in legal proceedings where the defendant's appearance is required, as a general principle bail shall be granted in keeping with the situation of the particular defendant–and with the understanding that confinement in circumstances where a person has not been convicted of a crime is an unjustified infringement of the rights of the person and an impediment to a defendant's having the best possible defense in the face of accusation and prosecution for alleged commission of a crime–except in cases where it is clearly demonstrated, through the appropriate legal proceeding, that releasing a defendant on bail poses an actual danger to the security of this Republic and its people. Denial of bail may be appealed, and such an appeal must be heard in a timely way–within 48 hours, except under extraordinary circumstances–by the appropriate court.

vii. Trials involving prosecution for criminal offenses shall be presided over by a judge, who shall have been appointed to that position in accordance with Article I, Section 3 and other relevant parts of this Constitution. The basic rules and procedures for criminal (and any other) legal proceedings shall be established by the appropriate legislative body. These rules and procedures must include: the right of defendants to the "presumption of innocence," that is, they may be convicted of a crime only if it is proven beyond a reasonable doubt that they are guilty of that crime (and juries shall be duly informed and reminded of this principle); the right of persons against self-incrimination, including the right not to testify in proceedings in which they are accused of violation of the law; and the right of defendants to have presented, in open court, all witnesses and evidence against them and the right (exercised directly by themselves and/or through the representation of legal counsel) to question and challenge all such witnesses and evidence. In keeping with the basic orientation articulated in Article I, Section 3, regarding the use of, and translation into, different languages in judicial proceedings, all defendants in criminal proceedings have the right to any assistance they may require from translators, in order to fully understand and participate in these legal proceedings and to fully exercise their rights in such proceedings. In criminal proceedings, the accused has the right to have a trial by a jury, selected from the general adult population of voting age in the relevant jurisdiction, in accordance with laws and procedures established in conformity with this Constitution. A defendant in a criminal case may also choose to forego a jury trial and to have the verdict rendered by a judge.

viii. The law and due process of law shall provide for appeal in cases of criminal conviction. With regard to the appeal process, the more serious the crime, the more that weight shall be given to providing avenues of appeal. Legal representation by the Department of Legal Defense and Assistance shall be provided, if requested by the defendants, or if ordered by a judge with the relevant authority, in appeals of criminal convictions.

ix. In regard to all those convicted and sentenced to be punished for violation of the law, the basic orientation with regard to such imprisonment shall be to rehabilitate the persons convicted and imprisoned, and to release them and reintegrate them as productive members of the larger society, as soon as it may be possible to do so, in accordance with the judgment that this can be done without unacceptable risk and danger to society and the people, and where doing so would not be contrary to what is set forth in this Constitution. To this end, education, in accordance with the principles set forth in this Constitution–and in particular the principle of "solid core, with a lot of elasticity," including education in the communist worldview and values but also access to a wide variety of political and philosophical, scientific, literary and other works, expressing a diversity of views–shall be afforded prisoners, and they shall be provided with the means to engage in productive work which can make a contribution to society, under conditions which are not only humane but which conform to the general standards of work in society at large. In no case shall persons be kept in prison for a period longer than that provided for by law and through legal proceedings embodying due process of law.

x. Cruel and unusual punishment, including torture, shall be prohibited.

xi. The New Socialist Republic in North America having been established and its organs of government–including the courts and other institutions dealing with justice, law and security–functional: from that time forward, the death penalty shall be eliminated and prohibited, except in circumstances of extraordinary emergency (as discussed in H, below). And once such circumstances of extraordinary emergency have been overcome, and the normal functioning of society and government can be resumed, the death penalty shall once again be prohibited. Even in circumstances of extraordinary emergency, a judgment of the death penalty shall be rendered only in extreme cases, and whenever possible the carrying out of this sentence shall be suspended pending the end of the extraordinary emergency, at which time the prohibition against the death penalty shall once again apply.

H. If, in its judgment, a situation of war, invasion or insurrection directed against the state, or other extraordinary circumstances, constitute a direct and immediate threat to the security, or even the very existence, of the New Socialist Republic in North America, the central Executive Council may declare a "security emergency" and, if it deems this necessary, may temporarily suspend rights and provisions set forth in this Article and elsewhere in this Constitution, including the prohibition of the death penalty. But, under no circumstances may torture or other means of cruel and unusual punishment be applied, and the principle of the humane treatment of prisoners, of all kinds, must be adhered to.

In the event of such suspension of certain rights and provisions of this Constitution, within the shortest possible time after such suspension–one week or less, unless circumstances absolutely prevent this, and in any case as soon as it can actually be done–this action by the Executive must be reviewed by the Supreme Court, which shall have the authority to determine whether any part of this action by the central Executive Council, or this action in its entirety, is actually required by the circumstances and is in accord with this Constitution. With regard to any parts of such an action, or the action as a whole, which the Supreme Court finds to be in violation of the Constitution: this must be immediately ended, upon such judgment. Further, until a normal situation and the normal functioning of society and government shall have resumed, a review by the Supreme Court of the actions and policies of the Executive in carrying out emergency measures, including the suspension of civil and legal rights and liberties, must be repeated, at regular intervals of no more than 30 days, to determine whether the circumstances continue to justify these policies and actions. Further, the central Legislature must be apprised of the reasons for this action by the Executive Council and must be convened to discuss this action and to offer its advice to the Executive Council, within the shortest possible time–not to exceed 15 days, if at all possible. The orientation and standard with regard to such emergencies must be: to restrict <u>only to the degree really necessary</u> the rights and liberties of the people during such emergencies, to put an end to such emergencies at the earliest possible time and, upon the ending of such emergencies, to fully restore the rights and liberties of the people, in accordance with what is set forth in this Constitution.

Section 3. Eradicating the Oppression of Women.

1. The oppression of women emerged thousands of years ago in human history together with the splitting of society into exploiting and exploited classes, and this oppression is one of the cornerstones of all societies based on exploitation. For the same reason, the struggle to finally and fully uproot the oppression of women is of profound importance and will be a decisive driving force in carrying forward the revolution toward the final goal of communism, and the eradication of all exploitation and oppression, throughout the world. Based on this understanding, the New Socialist Republic in North America gives the highest priority not only to establishing and giving practical effect to full legal equality for women–and to basic rights and liberties that are essential for the emancipation of women, such as reproductive freedom, including the right to abortion as well as birth control–but also to the increasing, and increasingly unfettered, involvement of women, equally with men, in every sphere of society, and to propagating and popularizing the need for and importance of uprooting and overcoming all remaining expressions and manifestations of patriarchy and male supremacy, in the economic and social relations and in the realms of politics, ideology and culture, and to promote the objective of fully emancipating women and the pivotal role of the struggle for this emancipation in the overall transformation of this society and the world as a whole. This orientation, and policies and laws flowing from it, shall be applied, promoted, encouraged and supported with the full political, legal and moral force, authority and influence of the government, at all levels, in the New Socialist Republic in North America.

Section 4. Uprooting National Oppression and Overcoming Gaps Between Regions and Other Great Differences.

1. As set forth in the preceding Article in this Constitution, the orientation, laws and policies of the government of the New Socialist Republic in North America shall also attach great

importance to–and shall wield to the fullest extent the political, legal and moral force, authority and influence of the government on behalf of–achieving the full equality of nationalities within this Republic and to overcoming the whole history and continuing effects of national oppression, not only in this society but throughout the world.

2. As evidenced in the historical experience of oppressed nationalities in the imperialist USA (and in experience throughout the world) overcoming inequalities between regions is closely interconnected with uprooting national oppression. Especially for this reason, the government of the New Socialist Republic in North America will devote special attention, efforts, and resources to the development of regions which, owing to the rule of exploiting classes and the dynamics of capitalism, and other factors, have been maintained, under the old system, in a more backward state, and to overcoming disparities between regions, as well as the gaps between urban and rural areas (in this regard see also Article IV).

Section 5. The Mental/Manual Contradiction.

1. Longstanding and deeply-rooted division between intellectual and physical work, and between those who primarily engage in the one and the other (the mental/manual contradiction), is bound up with the antagonistic division of society into exploiters and exploited, and itself contains the seeds of such antagonistic division. In order to continue developing the economy, and transforming not only the relations of production but the society as a whole, on the road of socialism toward the final goal of a communist world, it is necessary to correctly handle the contradictions that are bound up with, and interpenetrate with, this division–neither undermining the sphere of intellectual work nor reinforcing and perpetuating an oppressive division between intellectual and physical work–so as to finally move beyond a world in which such divisions exist and fetter human beings, and to bring into being a community of freely associating human beings who are capable of carrying out, and find fulfillment in carrying out, both physical and intellectual labor.

2. The orientation, laws, policies and actions of the government of the New Socialist Republic in North America shall give expression to these objectives and the struggle to achieve them.

Section 6.

What is set forth in the preceding Sections of this Article, together with the principles in the following Article (IV) regarding the development of the economy along socialist lines, is decisive in terms of the exercise of the most basic right of the people in this Republic and in the continuing struggle to finally uproot and move beyond all relations of exploitation and oppression, in this society and in the world as a whole—which is fundamental to, and must be at the heart of and a driving force in, the New Socialist Republic in North America. And in all this the leadership role of the Revolutionary Communist Party will be of decisive importance.

Article IV. The Economy and Economic Development in the New Socialist Republic in North America.

Section 1.

The economy of the New Socialist Republic in North America is a planned socialist economy, under the direction of the state and led by the Revolutionary Communist Party, in accordance with the principles and provisions set forth in Article I, Section 2 and elsewhere in this Constitution. Social production and economic development are guided and evaluated according to three overarching criteria:

1. Advancing the world revolution to uproot all exploitation and oppression and to emancipate all of humanity;

2. Meeting social need, creating a common material wealth that contributes to the all-around development of society and the individuals who make it up, and overcoming oppressive divisions between mental and manual labor, town and country, different regions and nationalities, and men and women;

3. Protecting, preserving, and enhancing the ecosystems and biodiversity of the planet for current and future generations.

Section 2.

Socialist production is based on and promotes relations and values of people working cooperatively for the common good and for the interests of world humanity. Socialist relations of production must enable the masses of people to gain increasing collective mastery over economic processes. In line with this orientation and these objectives, the exploitation of human labor, and the sale and purchase of labor power, is forbidden, except as this may be allowed and provided for, for a limited time on a transitional basis, and on a small scale, within the overall framework of socialist economic development and in accordance with socialist planning to effect such development.

Section 3.

In order to develop the economy along socialist lines it is necessary to put revolutionary politics in command of economic matters. To meet goals and solve problems of production, the state must mobilize the conscious activism of people in accordance with the principles and objectives set forth here and elsewhere in this Constitution. It must encourage initiative and creativity to advance the public interest.

Section 4.

1. A socialist economy operates according to principles of "socialist sustainable development." It takes the "long view" of what is needed to benefit humanity and the planet. It organizes and regulates production and growth on the basis of awareness of natural limits and the interconnected web of ecosystems. It emphasizes safe and renewable sources of energy.

2. The state in the New Socialist Republic in North America recognizes special internationalist responsibilities to share knowledge and technology, to allocate resources, and to promote initiatives to protect the global environment—and to assist the people in other parts of the world, especially in the Third World, to cope with the damage caused by imperialist environmental despoliation and plunder.

Section 5. The System of Public-State Ownership is the Foundation of the New Socialist Economy.

1. This form of ownership concentrates the highest interests of the proletariat and masses of people and the revolution which embodies those interests. It enables society to consciously and collectively utilize and develop social productive forces in order to transform society and the world and to enable humanity to truly become caretakers of the planet.

Means of production, and other private capital and wealth of the former capitalist-imperialist ruling class of the United States of America, shall be expropriated, without compensation, and converted into state/public property (or other forms of property which are in accordance with state planning and the development of the economy along socialist lines). With regard to others–who were not part of that ruling class and did not play an active role in opposing the revolution which led to the establishment of the New Socialist Republic in North America–means of production they own at the time of the founding of this Republic will be dealt with in the framework of overall state planning and the development of public-state ownership of the means of production, but appropriate compensation shall be provided to them for means of production owned by them which are converted to public-state ownership. In accordance with provisions established in law, they shall be entitled, for a certain period, to retain land (and houses and other property appertaining directly to this land) that they owned at the time of the founding of this Republic, up to a certain value, although they may not sell this land and related property– and it may be used only for personal purposes, and not as a means of production or other capital–except as authorized by state planning; after a period prescribed by law, the state may exercise the authority to acquire, with appropriate compensation, such land and other related property, converting it into public-state property, in line with the overall needs and development of the socialist economy. In conformity with these same basic principles and objectives, laws shall be established which make due allowance for the inheritance of personal property, within certain limits, while also ensuring that personal property is not converted into private capital, except as may be authorized by state planning, and that such inheritance and use of personal property does not come into fundamental conflict with and undermine the development of the economy, and the society overall, along the road of socialism.

2. The major means of production–factories and large-scale industrial-agricultural equipment, telecommunications, systems of transport, industrial-agricultural storage and distribution systems, etc., as well as land and raw materials–are state/public property (which for a time may be supplemented by cooperative and collective forms of ownership involving parts of the population, in accordance with state planning and in the overall context of socialist development of the economy), except where, also in accordance with state planning and in the overall context of socialist development, some private ownership of means of production may be allowed. The banking-financial system is state owned and directed.

3. Land, waters, forests, minerals, and other natural resources are protected and managed as "public goods." They fall within the scope of public-state ownership. Socialist-state ownership recognizes its responsibility to preserve the "commons"–the atmosphere, oceans, wildlife, and so forth–for all of humanity and for the future.

4. It is unlawful to turn public-state means of production into private property for speculation or to sell or purchase such means of production as private property. Destruction of state property and despoliation of natural resources is subject to punishment as prescribed by law and in accordance with due process of law.

5. The state in the New Socialist Republic in North America exercises firm control over all channels of foreign trade.

6. Collective-cooperative ownership is recognized as a secondary and transitional form of ownership applying to certain sectors of commerce, artisanal, and some small-scale, localized forms of agricultural and industrial production.

Section 6. The Socialist Economy Practices Comprehensive and Unified Planning.

1. The knowledge, skills, capabilities and resources of the people and the society are deployed to serve what is useful and important for the betterment of world humanity.

2. The socialist economy combines long- and short-term plans to guide development in accordance with conscious revolutionary goals. It seeks to correctly handle and balance long-term and more immediate interests.

3. Plans are drawn up, reviewed, and modified on the basis of consultation with the masses and through mass discussion, broad debate, and political struggle over the direction of society.

4. Plans must be implemented but must also be flexible and provide extensive leeway for adjustments and change.

5. The principle of "solid core, with a lot of elasticity" informs the system of economic planning. The planning system operates through mechanisms of centralization and decentralization. Centralization involves overall leadership in drawing up plans and in coordinating the economy; establishment of key economic, social, and environmental priorities; attention to major input-output requirements and technological, sectoral, regional, and ecological balances; centrally set prices and financial policy; unified principles of management; attention to overall coherence and direction of economic development and the needs of the world revolution. Decentralization involves local management and initiative, maximizing to the greatest degree possible collective participation and decision-making at the basic levels of society, and giving wide scope to experimentation and adaptation within the overall framework of the plan.

6. Individual units and enterprises of the socialist economy are integrated into the overall plan and must operate with a sense of larger social and global responsibility.

7. The dangers of bourgeois-bureaucratic methods of planning and "overgrowth of administration," on the one hand, and units, sectors, and lower levels "going their own way" independent of the highest interests of the revolution, on the other–these dangers must be put before society and combatted.

8. Socialist economic development is not undertaken as though it were a clockwork mechanism of coordination and control. Planning is led by a revolutionary line and is a process of struggle, transformation, discovery and learning–and is inseparable from

social movements and social struggles that emerge in response to the unresolved contradictions of socialist society.

9. The state in the New Socialist Republic in North America and the planned economy under its direction take special measures for "raising the bottom up." This principle serves the crucial task of overcoming historic inequalities affecting the formerly oppressed nationalities, and other profound disparities in society. The whole of society will be mobilized to overcome these inequalities. Priorities in distribution of needed social goods and services (like health and housing) will be guided by this principle. The socialist economy also gives priority to overcoming gaps between the more developed regions and areas and the less developed.

To redress the systematic dispossession of land and the ruination of farming livelihoods of Black and other minority farmers by the former capitalist-imperialist system, the government of the New Socialist Republic in North America will, for a certain period, allocate some farmland as private, individual/family property to those so affected and desiring to re-engage in this form of productive cultivation of land and allow for the continued private ownership/cultivation of farmland by those minority farmers who have maintained this mode of activity and wish to carry it on. This will be a transitional measure and will be carried out in the framework of the overall socialist development of the economy, which will be encouraged and fostered among farmers, as well as other sections of the people, in keeping with the reality that the socialist transformation of agriculture, and the economy as a whole, is fundamental to bringing into being a society, and world, in which the masses of people, including formerly oppressed Black and other minority farmers, will finally be free of oppression and relations of exploitation will finally be ended.

10. The socialist economy takes account of the special needs of women, while at the same time prohibiting and eliminating discrimination against women, and fosters the transformation of all patriarchal relations, values, and ways of thinking–with the aim of finally abolishing all such relations, values, and ways of thinking and fully emancipating women.

Section 7. Classes and Class Struggle Continue to Exist in Socialist Society.

1. For the reasons that have been spoken to in other parts of this Constitution, bourgeois relations are regenerated in socialist society; and newly engendered bourgeois forces will seek to restructure society in a capitalist direction.

2. It is the right and responsibility of people in this society to interrogate, debate, and wage struggle over the actual content of socialist-state ownership and planning and the political-ideological outlook and policies in command of social production and development.

Section 8. Employment and Work, Social Fabric, and Urban and Rural Relations.

1. The right to employment and income is guaranteed. The socialist economy enables individuals of diverse capabilities and inclinations to contribute to the development of a liberating society, and to gain in knowledge and capability. Economic-social planning strives to forge the conditions for meaningful and fulfilling work that links people and their creativity to each other and to the goal of emancipating humanity.

2. The allocation of social labor in the planned socialist economy combines volunteering with assignment to work and tasks, in order to meet the great needs of the new society and the advance of the world revolutionary struggle. People may volunteer, or apply, for work in various fields and areas of the economy and society, and while this will be taken into account to a significant degree, in an overall and ultimate sense decisions as to the allocation of work and the assignment of tasks must be made on the basis of the plan and the key principles of socialist economic development. The orientation of "mobilizing all positive factors"– unleashing the skills, innovativeness, and determination of broad strata of society and seeking to maximize the learning and interaction between different segments of society–will be applied. This takes place in an atmosphere in which the needs and priorities of society are broadly discussed, debated, and struggled out. On this basis, people will be increasingly motivated to voluntarily and consciously act in the larger public interest. At the same time,

allowance and provision will be made for various individuals as well as working groups to take initiative, and engage in creative exploration and experimentation, in the overall framework of and in fundamental accordance with the principles of socialist economic planning and the development of the economy, and the society as a whole, along socialist lines: this is an important principle and method with regard to the economy, as well as science and other spheres.

3. Members of the Revolutionary Communist Party must lead in going to the front lines and taking up the most difficult assignments and tasks.

4. The workplace is not simply a unit of production. The workplace is a site of politics, ideology and culture; it is a site of the struggle to remake society. Critical questions–from international affairs to educational policy, to the struggles to overcome national inequalities and to emancipate women–must be taken up.

5. The socialist economy seeks to overcome the numbing and alienating effects of the oppressive division of labor of the old capitalist society. Individuals in work units will have particular responsibilities, but will also rotate between positions and duties. Delegations from different units and sectors of the economy will carry on exchanges with other units and sectors. As revolution spreads and advances worldwide, such exchanges will be increasingly conducted on an international scale.

6. The socialist economy aims to break down walls between units of production and surrounding social life, and to combine work with residence and community. Economic-social planning strives to promote sustainable cities that thrive on a new kind of "social space" enabling people to meaningfully interact, organize politically, create and enjoy culture, recreate and relax. Economic-social planning seeks to integrate agriculture and industry, along with urban and rural activities, in new ways– and to connect people more closely with agricultural land and with nature.

7. Managers must take part in production; forms of collective management involving the direct producers must be established; and people as a whole will, increasingly, rotate between

administrative tasks and productive labor. Regulations and rules must serve the conscious social organization of production.

8. Citizens and legal residents have the right to strike, along with other basic rights that are set forth in Article III and elsewhere in this Constitution.

9. In matters of wages and income, the socialist state applies the broad principle: "From each according to her/his ability, to each according to her/his work." The specific categories and grades of wages and salaries are established centrally. A substantial portion of consumer goods will, for some time, be supplied through consumer markets; although these markets will be regulated by the state, consumption will still involve individual purchase and possession. The state protects the right of people to their income from work, savings, and other means of legal livelihood.

10. While instituting the socialist principle of payment for work, the socialist state strives, step-by-step, to reduce wage and salary differences. It leads struggle against backward values of competitive gain and self-enrichment and promotes the outlook of "serving the people" and advancing the revolution. It expands the sphere of distribution of goods and services, like housing and health care, according to social need and through more collective means (in workplaces, neighborhoods, etc.).

11. With regard to those who, owing to illness, injury, or disability, are unable to work in other capacities, they will be provided with opportunities to contribute to society and with the necessities of life, including intellectual and cultural as well as material needs, in keeping with the general standards prevailing in society overall; attention will be paid and resources devoted to their particular needs, while at the same time they will be integrated into the larger social and political life of society. The same basic approach will be applied to people who have reached the age of retirement. It is a matter of basic orientation and principle in a socialist state, such as the New Socialist Republic in North America, that, while all those who are of the appropriate ages, and are physically and mentally able to do so, shall work in order to earn their income–and, more fundamentally, in order to contribute to the development and transformation of society and the world as a whole, in keeping with

the principles set forth in this Constitution–all people, from the time of birth and throughout their lives, shall enjoy the full benefits and rights of living in such a state and, while taking into account the particular situations of different individuals, all shall be extended the fullest possible opportunities to be active and productive members of this society and to contribute to the fulfillment of its objectives. In keeping with this orientation, and with regard specifically to "the most vulnerable" in society, they shall have the right to have their most basic needs met–which includes a supportive social environment as well as essential material necessities–and to be integrated to the greatest degree possible into the flow of society. Besides the physically and mentally disabled, and the elderly, this shall be applied to those who, particularly in the early stages of this Republic, might be temporarily homeless or orphaned, and to any others in need of some form of supplemental assistance to most fully partake of, and to in turn enrich in many ways, the society at large and the new world being brought into being.

Section 9. The Socialist State as a Base Area for the World Revolution.

1. This orientation is built into the state's economic structures and its planning system and priorities, as well as its capacities to dispatch resources and people to different parts of the world to carry out various internationalist tasks and responsibilities.

2. In all international economic relations, proletarian internationalism and the needs of the world revolution come first.

3. With other socialist states that exist or come into being, trade will be carried out under the principles of proletarian internationalism, to aid the construction of socialism in these countries and the world revolution.

4. With regard to imperialist and reactionary states, the New Socialist Republic in North America will not put economic exchanges and agreements above its responsibility to support revolutionary movements in these countries.

5. Trade with nations and countries which remain under the domination and oppression of imperialism must also be

conducted on the basis of proletarian internationalism, and will take into account relations of dependency imposed by the former U.S. empire–requiring, in some cases, that parts, supplies, equipment and other assistance be provided to these countries for some time. But this must also take into account the nature of these countries and of their governments and ruling classes, the class struggle within them, and the role of these countries internationally.

6. The structure of production and the resource base of the socialist economy cannot depend on labor and materials from other countries–much less exploitation and domination. The development of a socialist economy must not involve the export of capital–for example, building factories, or making loans, for profit. A socialist economy must not reproduce relations of domination and inequality in its international interactions. This question, too, must be put before the masses of people, as part of their coming to more deeply understand, and to act on, the basic principles on which the New Socialist Republic in North America is founded and according to which it must proceed.

7. A socialist economy must practice self-reliance and sustainability at the same time that it aids the struggles of the exploited and oppressed of the world.

8. The economy must be planned and developed in such a way as to make provision for, and actually provide, the resources and technology necessary for the security and defense of the society and the state against provocations, aggression and attacks by imperialists and other reactionary forces. At the same time, this must be done in accordance with the principles set forth in this Constitution–including specifically those regarding defense and security–and without allowing the provision of the necessary means for defense and security to fundamentally distort or undermine the development of the economy, and the society overall, along socialist lines and the fulfilling of internationalist responsibilities. The armed forces must, at all levels, strive to economize on expenditure and, where possible and in correspondence with overall economic planning, engage in productive activities that can contribute to their self-provisioning.

Section 10. The Socialist Economy and the Advance to Communism.

1. The system of ownership, the relations among people in production, and the distribution of the products of human labor reflect the material and ideological development of socialist society. But they must undergo change through continuing revolution and contribute in their motion and development to furthering the revolutionary struggle to achieve a higher level of society–communism–throughout the world.

2. In communist society, the enslaving subordination of the individual to the division of labor will be overcome; commodity production and exchange through money will be replaced with the direct distribution of social products, on the basis of overall planning; the principle of "from each according to his/her abilities, to each according to his/her needs" will guide distribution on the basis of a leap in the material and ideological development of society; and a higher form of social ownership and planning, no longer requiring the mediation of a state, will be achieved.

3. Socialist society, and the economy which is its foundation, must be moving, and be led, in this direction–toward the goal of communism. The planned socialist economy must nurture the seeds of the communist transformation and reorganization of the world.

Article V. Adoption of This Constitution.

Section 1.

This Constitution had been distributed, and discussion and debate in regard to it promoted, for a whole period, by the Revolutionary Communist Party, as one key element in building a movement for revolution; and then, with the qualitative change in the situation and the emergence of the necessary conditions, this was done in connection with the struggle that resulted in the defeat and dismantling of the imperialist forces of the USA, and their state apparatus of violence and repression, and the founding of the New Socialist Republic in North America.

This Constitution shall have been adopted, in the first instance, by the Provisional Governing Council established under the leadership of the Revolutionary Communist Party, after the existence of the New Socialist Republic in North America had been declared by an official statement of the Party. This Provisional Governing Council shall have been convened, and deliberated and decided on this Constitution, in as expeditious a manner as possible, in keeping with the immediate need to establish the new revolutionary state on a clear and firm constitutional foundation. Members of this Council shall have been drawn from those directly taking part in, as well as those actively supporting, the revolutionary struggle that resulted in the founding of this Republic, but it shall also have involved others from diverse strata among the people. After discussion of the Preamble and the various Articles of this Constitution, this Council shall have approved and adopted this Constitution (with any changes it deemed necessary and appropriate) by a simple majority vote of its members.

Section 2.

Having been adopted by the Provisional Governing Council referred to in Section 1, this Constitution shall have force and be in effect throughout the New Socialist Republic in North America.

Article VI. Amendments to This Constitution.

Section 1.

Amendments to this Constitution may be proposed, and the process of considering such amendments initiated, by the central Legislature or the legislatures in the regions, including any autonomous regions (or other autonomous areas) that may be established, and in the localities of this Republic. This process may also be initiated through proposals made by the central Executive Council.

Section 2.

1. In the case of amendments that are raised directly in the central Legislature, by one or more of its members, the matter

shall be decided by a vote of that body. If at least 3/4 of the members of that Legislature vote in favor of the amendment, it shall then be prepared as a referendum to be voted on in a general election, in the same manner, and according to the same basic apportioned procedures, as shall apply to the election of the central Legislature, as set forth in Article I, Section 1–with the difference that is contained in point 2 below.

2. If this referendum is affirmed by at least 2/3 of the votes cast in accordance with the procedures discussed in point 1 above, the amendment shall be adopted, and shall become part of this Constitution, within 30 days after this vote has been tabulated and the final result announced.

3. In the case of amendments which are proposed by the central Executive Council, they shall be presented to the central Legislature, and then the matter shall be voted on by this central Legislature–and if approved by at least 3/4 of the members of that Legislature, the matter shall then proceed in accordance with what is set forth above in this Section of this Article.

4. In the case of amendments which are proposed by a member (or members) of the legislature of a region, including an autonomous region (or other autonomous area), or a locality, the amendments shall first be voted on by the legislature in question. If at least 2/3 of the members of that legislature vote in support of such a proposed amendment, it shall then be presented to the central Legislature, and from there things shall proceed in accordance with what is set forth above in this Section of this Article.